The NO-NONSENSE GUIDE to
INDIGENOUS PEOPLES

'Publishers have created lists of short books that discuss the questions that your average [electoral] candidate will only ever touch if armed with a slogan and a soundbite. Together [such books] hint at a resurgence of the grand educational tradition... Closest to the hot headline issues are *The No-Nonsense Guides*. These target those topics that a large army of voters care about, but that politicos evade. Arguments, figures and documents combine to prove that good journalism is far too important to be left to (most) journalists.'

Boyd Tonkin,
The Independent,
London

About the author

Lotte Hughes is an historian of Africa and empire, who works largely on Kenya. She is based at The Ferguson Centre for African and Asian Studies, The Open University, UK. Her doctoral research was on Maasai land alienation in colonial Kenya (University of Oxford, 2002), later published as *Moving the Maasai: A Colonial Misadventure* (Palgrave Macmillan, 2006). She is currently researching heritage and memory issues in contemporary Kenya. She previously worked as a journalist, and has written about world development and human rights issues for newspapers and NGOs.

The **NO-NONSENSE GUIDE** to

INDIGENOUS PEOPLES

Lotte Hughes

New Internationalist

BTL

The No-Nonsense Guide to Indigenous Peoples, Second Edition
Published in Canada by
New Internationalist™ Publications Ltd.   and   Between the Lines
2446 Bank Street, Suite 653   401 Richmond Street West,
Ottawa, Ontario   Studio 277
K1V 1A8   Toronto, Ontario
www.newint.org   M5V 3A8
                                                                   www.btlbooks.com

First published in the UK by
New Internationalist™ Publications Ltd
55 Rectory Road
Oxford OX4 1BW
New Internationalist is a registered trade mark.

© Lotte Hughes/New Internationalist 2012

Series editor: Chris Brazier
Design by New Internationalist Publications Ltd

Printed in Canada

Library and Archives Canada Cataloguing in Publication

Hughes, Lotte
     The no-nonsense guide to indigenous peoples / Lotte Hughes. -- 2nd ed.

(The no-nonsense guides)
Includes index.
Co-published by New Internationalist.
Issued also in electronic formats.
ISBN 978-1-926662-96-1

     1. Indigenous peoples. I. Title.
II. Series: No-nonsense guides (Toronto, Ont.)

GN380.H83 2012   305.8   C2011-907731-0

Between the Lines gratefully acknowledges assistance for its publishing
activities from the Canada Council for the Arts, the Ontario Arts Council, the
Government of Ontario through the Ontario Book Publishers Tax Credit program
and through the Ontario Book Initiative, and the Government of Canada
through the Canada Book Fund.

Foreword

THE HISTORY OF THE WORLD is inseparable from the fate of indigenous peoples. From Australia to Amazonia, groups who occupied the fertile shores and river valleys have been pushed into far, infertile corners of their own worlds, or exterminated by explorers, colonizers and nation states. This means that the morality of our world is also bound up in their fate. How a 'modern' state views and deals with aboriginal peoples is revealing. The survivors may be in 'remote' arid, icy or hidden landscapes, but their significance lies at the center, not the periphery, of our world.

Lotte Hughes' remarkable book charts the histories and politics of indigenous societies. Some issues are complicated and unresolved: the notion of 'indigenous' is full of contention, with a maze of definitions. A strength of this *Guide* is that it acknowledges difficulties and refuses deconstruction, without obscuring the variety and complexity of indigenous societies.

The *Guide* describes the achievements, as well as the grief and oppression. It highlights the key feature of indigenous systems: a nurturing, respectful relationship to the land. Indigenous peoples wish to ensure that the land they use and the creatures they kill to eat will continue to sustain them. This is revealed in a fascinating intersection between religious and material relationships to the world. Many Europeans have taken inspiration from this, sometimes being derided as naïve and romantic. For indigenous peoples can be just as ruthless with their environment or with one another as the rest of us. In addressing romanticism, Lotte Hughes points out that indigenous societies need the world around them to stay the same: survival depends on the land and animals remaining as they are, with only minor changes. To note this is not to romanticize but to report social and economic realities. Environmental conservatism does not make people 'good', or mean they are without human cruelties – but it does mean that they have tended to be good environmentalists. It also means that they have expertise that can benefit not just local territories, but all peoples.

The success of their environmentalism makes their displacement all the more poignant. For loss of land usually means the loss of the possibility to be themselves. They rely on the territory: where ancestors have nurtured the earth, cared for the animals, propitiated the spirits. A cruel irony of their displacement is that they have often been accused, by those wishing to displace them, of killing too many animals, over-fishing or neglecting the land. Hence many groups have been forced out of national parks in east and southern Africa, despite having ensured, by their customs and skills, the enduring beauty and abundance of these places. Elsewhere, mines, forestry and intensive agriculture have dispossessed so many.

But this *Guide* also tells of the fight back. Indigenous groups have formed international alliances, and have a permanent presence at the UN. They are battling to secure rights to live on their lands, to check logging, to preserve fisheries, to manage their own resources and to take effective part in government. These struggles may be versions of David and Goliath, without promise of miraculous outcome. But there have been successes. The challenge now is for indigenous peoples to define, and the rest of the world to respect, a development model that is neither an unrealistic ideal of times gone nor an acceptance of final assimilation in colonial nation states. Indigenous peoples ask that their voices be heard, their stories be told and that they take their place, on their own terms, in their own lands. This *No-Nonsense Guide* lays out the issues behind and within this challenge.

Hugh Brody
Anthropologist, filmmaker and author of *Maps and Dreams* and *The Other Side of Eden*

CONTENTS

Introduction

SINCE THIS BOOK was first published in 2003, there has been a sea-change in the world of indigenous peoples and their rights.

The most significant change was the adoption in 2007, by the United Nations General Assembly, of the UN Declaration on the Rights of Indigenous Peoples. This followed more than two decades of dialogue, and represents (in the words of the indigenous rights' organization Cultural Survival) 'a blueprint for how Indigenous People worldwide should be treated'. However, the Declaration has yet to be fully implemented, and the struggle continues to see its provisions, described in 46 articles, applied internationally.

The first International Decade of the World's Indigenous People (1995-2004) has come and gone, and a second Decade began in January 2005. Indigenous peoples' rights have become an increasingly important subject in international law, and a series of landmark legal judgments has broken new ground. As the result of emerging rights regimes, the establishment at the UN of a Permanent Forum on Indigenous Issues, the widening of democratic space and flowering of civil society in many countries, together with the proliferation of international and national development agencies, we have witnessed a surge in indigenous activism and advocacy.

A global indigenous rights industry has arisen, the effects of which are not always positive. Groups are fiercely competing for donor funds and other resources, and some of the poorest communities – who may lack access to power-brokers and policy-makers – can be marginalized in the process. On the plus side, indigenous activists have been able to influence policy-making – on issues such as environmental management and tourism on indigenous lands – and continue trying to ensure that indigenous peoples' needs and rights are taken into account.

Some of the most striking changes have come about in South America, not least in Bolivia, which, since 2006, has had, in the form of Evo Morales, its first indigenous president. Domestically he has introduced policies benefiting indigenous communities through land reforms and redistribution of wealth, while, on the international stage, in climate negotiations, President Morales has argued from an indigenous perspective for greater respect to be shown to 'Mother Earth'.

Another fascinating development is the phenomenon of 'becoming indigenous'. This refers to the attempt by certain communities to reconstruct and present themselves as indigenous people, when they may not meet the widely accepted criteria. While understandable, in parts of the world where identities and claims are increasingly politicized and essentialized, and where people are competing for dwindling resources, this can be highly problematic.

This book tries to avoid romanticizing indigenous peoples, which some of the literature tends to do. I have tried to strike a balance between, for example, focusing on victimization and successful struggle; too much emphasis can often be put on the former, and not enough on how people have fought back. Rather than paint too rosy a picture of indigenous life and knowledge, I have also described tensions and contradictions. Indigenous people demand the right to speak for themselves, and this *No-Nonsense Guide* includes as many direct voices as possible.

All the communities mentioned in these pages deserve a book in their own right. It is impossible to include everyone and, in such a small space, to do justice to all the peoples, historical milestones and events that could be covered. Our aim is to provide illustrative snapshots, in the hope that readers will be inspired to find out more.

Lotte Hughes, November 2011

1 Who are indigenous peoples?

What is the difference between indigenous peoples, tribal peoples and minorities? And what does 'indigenous' actually mean? Where and how indigenous peoples live – and how they made a breakthrough at the United Nations.

A MIDDLE-AGED AMERICAN woman tourist and a young Maasai man bumped into each other at the entrance of a luxury hotel in Tanzania's Ngorongoro reserve. It was late 1983, and my Maasai friend Taté held a copy of George Orwell's novel *Nineteen Eighty-Four*, which he happened to be reading. He was dressed in a red toga-like garment (*shuka*) and adorned with beaded jewelry, looking every inch a 'man of the bush' – yet carrying a symbol of modernity and literacy.

The tourist timidly asked Taté in pidgin English, raising her camera: 'Can-I-take-your-picture?' My friend coolly looked her up and down. With some amusement he said, in perfect American-accented English acquired from US missionary teachers: 'Only if you are paying in US dollars, lady.' She fled, embarrassed, without taking a photo.

What does this exchange say about the way we often treat indigenous people? The tourist clearly assumed that Taté did not understand English. She did not notice the book, or perhaps not being a lover of literature, maybe did not know what it was. She probably thought him decorative and exotic, and with the best will in the world, wanted to capture his picture to take home and show the folks (as perhaps many of us have done). It would end up alongside photos of lions and jungles, part of a gallery of images of wild Africa. He, meanwhile, had other ideas. Tourists are welcome in Ngorongoro because they bring much-needed money. But since Maasai communities were forced out of the crater some years ago to make way for tourism and 'conservation' (Ngorongoro is an extinct volcano's caldera), they have not seen many direct benefits of either activity. They were, and are, fed up with being treated like human animals in a zoo – and widely seen as dumb and stupid, too. If she wanted his photo, he wanted to make a dollar on the deal. He thought the whole thing quite amusing; she was just confused. They were beings from completely different worlds, colliding in space and bruised by the collision. The story of indigenous peoples mirrors this one in many ways, but their struggle for recognition is usually much more serious, and the collision a lot more painful.

Definitions

Indigenous peoples are generally referred to in the plural, because there are many different groups who make up the entire global tapestry of indigenous peoples. The use of plural indicates the diversity of people within the group as a whole.

People do not agree on definitions, and in fact there is no unambiguous definition of the concept. Indigenous peoples themselves claim the right to define who they are, and reject the idea that outsiders can do so. They argue that self-identification as indigenous is one of their basic rights. Nevertheless anthropologists, for example, tend to use the term indigenous peoples to describe a non-dominant group in a particular territory, with a more or less acknowledged claim to be aboriginal – a word now used (with an initial capital letter) for the indigenous peoples of Australia in particular. But in its broadest sense, aboriginal simply means 'original inhabitants'. They are the people who were there first, who may also call themselves First Peoples or First Nations.

Indigenous, *a*. 1646. [f. L. *indigena* + -OUS; see prec.] **1**. Born or produced naturally in a land or region; native *to* (the soil, region, etc.). b. *transf.* and *fig.* Inborn, innate 1864. **2**. Native, vernacular 1844. *The Shorter Oxford English Dictionary.*

Who are indigenous peoples?

The Aboriginal peoples of Australia were undoubtedly there first, and the same is true of other groups such as the Maya of Guatemala, Central America, and certain (some would say all) African peoples. But in some places the issue is not always so clear cut. Neither is it clear cut within Africa where, for example, nomadic migrants from the north of the continent displaced other early peoples from territories further south which the incomers later claimed as their ancestral lands. Though an indigenous people may have arrived in a particular territory before other ethnic groups, there is a problem with the word 'first'. In some cases, who knows who got there first? The history of the world is the story of human migration – successive waves of people moving here and there, displacing other populations as they moved, conquered and occupied new territory. When you start digging, as archeologists have, you find that the terms 'original' and 'first' are not always strictly accurate. Other communities can claim to be first-comers, or to have arrived in the same region simultaneously. But some of those first-comers – like the Arawaks of the Caribbean island of Hispaniola – are now extinct, so they cannot speak for themselves.

It may be safer to say that indigenous peoples arrived in a territory before single nation states were formed, though to complicate matters this is equally true of some other communities who do not self-identify as indigenous, such as the Kikuyu of Kenya. Also, some indigenous peoples such as Native Americans were organized as sovereign nations long before European colonists arrived; for example, the Iroquois Confederacy comprised six nations and operated a highly structured state system.

However, these nations did not form single nation states as we know them today.[1] The International Work Group for Indigenous Affairs (IWGIA) gives this definition, as part of a longer one:

'Indigenous peoples are the disadvantaged descendants of those peoples that inhabited a territory prior to the formation of a state. The term indigenous may be defined as a characteristic relating the identity of a particular people to a particular area and distinguishing them culturally from other people or peoples. When, for example, immigrants from Europe settled in the Americas and Oceania, or when new states were created after colonialism was abolished in Africa and Asia, certain peoples became marginalized and discriminated against because their language, their religion, their culture and their whole way of life were different, and perceived by the dominant society as being inferior. Insisting on their right to self-determination is indigenous peoples' way of overcoming these obstacles. Today many indigenous peoples are still excluded from society and often even deprived of their rights as equal citizens of a state.'[2]

Indigenous peoples are often defined as 'non-state' and their mode of life and economy is not industrialized. This makes them vulnerable; they tend to be marginalized, which means pushed to the margins of society. This does not mean to say that individuals cannot be members of governments and parliaments, help to run the country, or work in factories. But generally speaking they are not at the head of things, running states and industry.

'Tribal peoples' can mean much the same thing. The major difference is that they do not or cannot always claim to be descended from the aboriginal inhabitants of a territory. Also, the word 'tribal', like 'tribe', can be insulting to some, and so is best avoided unless people choose to describe themselves this way. The word tribe is acceptable in the US, where it refers to a group of Native Americans who share a common language and culture, but is only acceptable in a few areas of Canada.

Many minorities are also indigenous, but not necessarily so. Examples of minority groups who are indigenous are the Karen of Burma (Myanmar) and the Yanomami of Brazil. Examples of minorities who are not indigenous are Korean Americans, British

Who are indigenous peoples?

Asians and Jehovah's Witnesses (unless individuals also happen to be members of indigenous groups). Surprisingly, there is no internationally agreed definition of minorities. The UN Declaration on Minorities covers 'national or ethnic, religious and linguistic' minorities, but in more than 65 years the UN has never agreed a definition of what constitutes a minority. The organization Minority Rights Group International (MRG) says minorities are 'often among the poorest and most marginalized groups in society. They may lack access to political power and frequently have development policies imposed on them.' MRG's work focuses on non-dominant ethnic, linguistic or religious communities who may not necessarily be in a numerical minority. These can include indigenous and tribal peoples as well as migrants and refugees. But such communities may not want to be classified as minorities, largely because the word 'minority' often has a negative connotation.

Official definitions

For official definitions of indigenous and tribal peoples, one must start by turning to the International Labour Organization (ILO) Convention No 169 Concerning Indigenous and Tribal Peoples in Independent Countries, which came into force in 1991. The ILO distinguishes indigenous from tribal peoples in the following way, saying the Convention applies to:

- Tribal peoples in independent countries whose social, cultural and economic conditions distinguish them from other sections of the national community and whose status is regulated wholly or partially by their own customs or traditions or by special laws or regulations;
- Peoples in independent countries who are regarded as indigenous on account of their descent from the populations which inhabited the country, or a geographical region to which the country belongs,

at the time of conquest or colonization or the establishment of present state boundaries and who, irrespective of their legal status, retain some or all of their own social, economic, cultural or political institutions;

- Self-identification as indigenous or tribal shall be regarded as a fundamental criterion for determining the groups to which the provisions of this Convention apply.[3]

This is still often cited in the absence of a clear United Nations (UN) definition since, although it has now adopted a Declaration on their Rights, the UN does not have an official definition of indigenous peoples. The other two widely used definitions were suggested by UN rapporteurs Dr José R Martinéz Cobo and Mme Erica-Irene Daes, and are called after the names of their creators. In his 1986 Report for the UN Sub-Commission on the Prevention of Discrimination and Protection of Minorities, Dr Martinéz Cobo wrote:

'Indigenous communities, peoples and nations are those which, having a historical continuity with pre-invasion and pre-colonial societies that developed on their territories, consider themselves distinct from other sectors of the societies now prevailing in those territories, or parts of them. They form at present non-dominant sectors of society and are determined to preserve, develop and transmit to future generations their ancestral territories, and their ethnic identity, as the basis of their continued existence as peoples, in accordance with their own cultural patterns, social institutions and legal systems.'[4]

Erica-Irene Daes, Chairperson of the UN Working Group on Indigenous Populations, suggested this variation, designating certain peoples as indigenous:

- because they are descendants of groups which were in the territory of the country at the time when other groups of different cultures or ethnic origins arrived there;
- because of their isolation from other segments of the

country's population they have preserved almost intact the customs and traditions of their ancestors which are similar to those characterized as indigenous; and
- because they are, even if only formally, placed under a State structure which incorporates national, social and cultural characteristics alien to theirs.[5]

In general, though, there is an increasing reluctance on the part of the UN system to come up with a specific and 'official' definition of indigenous peoples. There is a sense in which any such definition would inevitably include or exclude some people and might be applicable to some countries or cultures but not to others, thereby proving counter-productive.

The World Bank takes a similar line. Its official position is that 'because of the varied and changing contexts in which indigenous peoples live and because there is no universally accepted definition of indigenous peoples, this policy does not define the term. Indigenous peoples may be referred to in different countries by such terms as "indigenous ethnic minorities", "aboriginals", "hill tribes", "minority nationalities", "scheduled tribes", or "tribal groups".'[6]

This is not just bureaucratic caution. It broadly reflects the preference of indigenous peoples themselves, who consider that they, rather than officialdom, should be the ones doing the defining. Even the UN Declaration on the Rights of Indigenous Peoples, which was approved by the General Assembly in September 2007, contains no specific definition. Instead, Article 33 states:

1. Indigenous peoples have the right to determine their own identity or membership in accordance with their customs and traditions. This does not impair the right of indigenous individuals to obtain citizenship of the States in which they live.

2. Indigenous peoples have the right to determine the structures and to select the membership of their institutions in accordance with their own procedures.

The lack of a definition has not proved problematic

in other areas of UN policy – there has never been an official definition of a 'people' or of a 'minority', still less of 'terrorism', yet the UN has never been constrained from using these terms or from acting upon them.

But while the indigenous movement worldwide has called for self-identification to be the main criterion for identifying indigenous peoples, some national governments reject the whole principle of self-identification. For example, the Indian government has not signed or ratified ILO Convention 169 and refuses to recognize the Adivasis or 'scheduled tribes' as indigenous. It claims that the whole population of India is indigenous. Other governments have said much the same thing. For example, when the UN declared 1993 the Year of Indigenous Peoples and various organizations asked the Botswana government what this might mean for the country's San population, a minister retorted: 'All Batswana are indigenous.' It did not, therefore, see any need to make special arrangements for the minority San. The government was also trying to emphasize the equality of all its peoples, and to defend the non-discriminatory principles of the constitution.

This opens up an interesting debate. In countries vulnerable to ethnic strife, whose governments may be working hard to achieve non-racialism and equality for all, is it justifiable to privilege one ethnic group over others, just because they claim indigenous status and demand special attention? On the other hand, given their vulnerability, marginalization and extreme oppression, it is recognized that indigenous peoples have particular collective as well as individual rights that afford them a specified level and quality of protection under international human rights law – just as women, children, refugees and certain other marginalized groups do.

It is vital to stress that indigenous peoples demand recognition of their collective rights. The UN's Universal Declaration of Human Rights (1948) established the

Who are indigenous peoples?

principle of universal rights for all, but emphasized individual rights. This resulted in states (where they abided by it at all) assigning rights to individual citizens, and sometimes dismissing the validity of collective rights based on cultural, ethnic or other forms of group identity. For example, in the Nordic countries, the Sami's demand for collective rights is based on their status as one people. With the establishment of national Sami parliaments in Finland, Norway and Sweden, states that had previously favored individual rights finally recognized the principle of Sami group rights. This marked a major shift in attitude.

None of these issues is easy. People disagree constantly over terminology, never mind action or lack of it. Some scholars argue that the word 'indigenous' should be dropped altogether, because it is – like the concept of tribes – 'essentialist', which means reducing people and things to universally fixed essences. When applied to people, the theory of essentialism denies historical change and fluidity, the hallmark of human life itself.

Working definitions

Below is a summary of the main definitions.

- Indigenous peoples are non-dominant, non-state groups in a particular territory, who claim to be aboriginal (descended from the pre-colonial inhabitants). They identify themselves as indigenous and are regarded as such by others. They have distinct social, political and cultural identities, and languages, traditions, legal and political institutions that are distinct from those of the national society. They have a special relationship with the land and natural resources, which is often fundamental to their cultural identity and therefore their survival as distinct peoples. They are not industrialized, often subsistence producers, and they tend to be marginalized by wider society.

- Tribal peoples are much the same as indigenous, but they do not or cannot always claim to be descended from the original inhabitants of a territory. 'Tribal', like tribe, can be insulting, so the term is best avoided unless people choose to describe themselves this way.
- First Peoples, First Nations or First Nations people are those who claim to be descended from the original inhabitants of a territory.
- Minorities are people who are in the minority in the country where they live, but not necessarily numerically. They can be non-dominant for ethnic, linguistic or religious reasons. They can include indigenous peoples.
- The Fourth World was a term used by the World Council of Indigenous Peoples (the organization no longer exists) to distinguish the lifestyles of indigenous peoples from those of the so-called First World (highly industrialized nations), Second World (the former communist bloc) and the Third World (developing nations).

A useful rule of thumb is to consider how people prefer to describe themselves.

Indigenous peoples claim the right to define what is meant by indigenous, and to have other people recognize them as such. This *Guide* uses generic regional names such as Aboriginal, though there are often many subgroups within each indigenous population. Largely for reasons of space, the book does not give all these different names. There is no universally agreed lexicon that covers every group, so it is best to ask people what name they prefer. In the US, for example, people tend to align themselves with particular nations, such as the Mohawk Nation, also known as Kanien Kaha:ka.

Indigenous world

There are at least 7,000 indigenous societies around the world – though some put this figure much lower, at nearer 5,000, because they do not list different

A guide to some preferred names:		
Native Americans or First Nations	*not*	*Indians*
Aboriginal peoples, First Peoples, First Nations or First Nations people (nb First Nations excludes mixed-ancestry Métis, and Inuit. Indian is used in Canada to describe indigenous people who are not Inuit or Métis)	*not*	*Native Canadians*
Inuit	*not*	*Eskimo*
San	*not*	*Bushmen*
Mbuti, Efe, Lese, etc	*not*	*Pygmies*

subgroups, or because they exclude groups that do not fit the official working definitions of indigenous. Hard figures are difficult to come by because censuses are not reliable – different subgroups are sometimes not included and governments apply different criteria to establish who is indigenous and who is not. Current estimates put the number of indigenous peoples worldwide at somewhere around 370 million people, distributed between 90 countries.[7]

United Nations initiatives

The UN set up a Working Group on Indigenous Populations in 1982. One of its main tasks was to set standards, by drawing up a Draft Declaration on the Rights of Indigenous Peoples.

1995 marked the start of the UN's International Decade of the World's Indigenous Peoples. Unusually, the UN General Assembly decided to dedicate a second decade to indigenous peoples, which was to run from 2005 to 2014. A milestone was reached in December 2000 when the UN created a Permanent Forum on Indigenous Issues. This spelled victory for indigenous peoples who had struggled for decades to win official recognition in the global community.

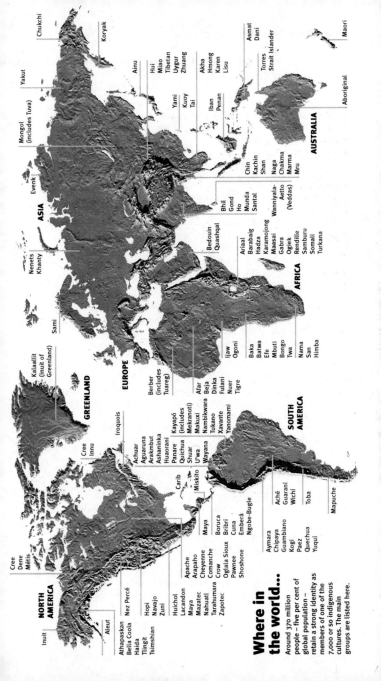

Where in the world...

Around 370 million people – five per cent of global population – retain a strong identity as members of one of the 7,000 or so indigenous cultures. The main groups are listed here.

UN Declaration on the Rights of Indigenous Peoples

The Declaration has 46 Articles. The first 14 of these are:

1 Indigenous peoples have the right to the full enjoyment, as a collective or as individuals, of all human rights and fundamental freedoms as recognized in the Charter of the United Nations, the Universal Declaration of Human Rights and international human rights law.

2 Indigenous peoples and individuals are free and equal to all other peoples and individuals and have the right to be free from any kind of discrimination, in the exercise of their rights, in particular that based on their indigenous origin or identity.

3 Indigenous peoples have the right to self-determination. By virtue of that right they freely determine their political status and freely pursue their economic, social and cultural development.

4 Indigenous peoples, in exercising their right to self-determination, have the right to autonomy or self-government in matters relating to their internal and local affairs, as well as ways and means for financing their autonomous functions.

5 Indigenous peoples have the right to maintain and strengthen their distinct political, legal, economic, social and cultural institutions, while retaining their right to participate fully, if they so choose, in the political, economic, social and cultural life of the State.

6 Every indigenous individual has the right to a nationality.

7 1. Indigenous individuals have the rights to life, physical and mental integrity, liberty and security of person.

2. Indigenous peoples have the collective right to live in freedom, peace and security as distinct peoples and shall not be subjected to any act of genocide or any other act of violence, including forcibly removing children of the group to another group.

8 1. Indigenous peoples and individuals have the right not to be subjected to forced assimilation or destruction of their culture.

2. States shall provide effective mechanisms for prevention of, and redress for:

(a) Any action which has the aim or effect of depriving them of their integrity as distinct peoples, or of their cultural values or ethnic identities;

(b) Any action which has the aim or effect of dispossessing them of their lands, territories or resources;

(c) Any form of forced population transfer which has the aim or effect of violating or undermining any of their rights;

(d) Any form of forced assimilation or integration;

(e) Any form of propaganda designed to promote or incite racial or ethnic discrimination directed against them.

9 Indigenous peoples and individuals have the right to belong to an indigenous community or nation, in accordance with the traditions and customs of the community or nation concerned. No discrimination of any kind may arise from the exercise of such a right.

10 Indigenous peoples shall not be forcibly removed from their lands or territories. No relocation shall take place without the free, prior and informed consent of the indigenous peoples concerned and after agreement on just and fair compensation and, where possible, with the option of return.

11 1. Indigenous peoples have the right to practice and revitalize their cultural traditions and customs. This includes the right to maintain, protect and develop the past, present and future manifestations of their cultures, such as archeological and historical sites, artefacts, designs, ceremonies, technologies and visual and performing arts and literature.

2. States shall provide redress through effective mechanisms, which may include restitution, developed in conjunction with indigenous peoples, with respect to their cultural, intellectual, religious and spiritual property taken without their free, prior and informed consent or in violation of their laws, traditions and customs.

12 1. Indigenous peoples have the right to manifest, practice, develop and teach their spiritual and religious traditions, customs and ceremonies; the right to maintain, protect, and have access in privacy to their religious and cultural sites; the right to the use and control of their ceremonial objects; and the right to the repatriation of their human remains.

2. States shall seek to enable the access and/or repatriation of ceremonial objects and human remains in their possession through fair, transparent and effective mechanisms developed in conjunction with indigenous peoples concerned.

13 1. Indigenous peoples have the right to revitalize, use, develop and transmit to future generations their histories, languages, oral traditions, philosophies, writing systems and literatures, and to designate and retain their own names for communities, places and persons.

2. States shall take effective measures to ensure that this right is protected and also to ensure that indigenous peoples can understand and be understood in political, legal and administrative proceedings, where necessary through the provision of interpretation or by other appropriate means.

14 1. Indigenous peoples have the right to establish and control their educational systems and institutions providing education in their own languages, in a manner appropriate to their cultural methods of teaching and learning.

2. Indigenous individuals, particularly children, have the right to all levels and forms of education of the State without discrimination.

3. States shall, in conjunction with indigenous peoples, take effective measures, in order for indigenous individuals, particularly children, including those living outside their communities, to have access, when possible, to an education in their own culture and provided in their own language.

Read the preamble and all 46 Articles in full at un.org/esa/socdev/unpfii/en/drip.html. ■

Who are indigenous peoples?

The 16-member Forum, which held its first session in May 2002 and is an advisory body to the UN Economic and Social Council, formally brings indigenous peoples and their representatives into the UN structure. For the first time, this has allowed representatives of states and non-state groups to enjoy equal status in a permanent representative body at the UN – eight of the members are nominated by governments and eight by indigenous peoples. Before, there was no permanent mechanism in the UN system to address the problems facing indigenous peoples. Since 2008, the Forum has expanded its mandate to include promoting respect for and the full application of the UN Declaration on the Rights of Indigenous Peoples.

The Declaration had a long and rather tortuous birth. Work on a draft began in 1985 but then went through a series of UN committees and redrafting processes over the next 20 years. There were disputes over whether or not some national governments would agree to the words 'peoples' or 'a people' to refer to indigenous peoples. There were also disagreements over whether to use the terms 'territory', 'land rights', 'self-determination' and 'self-government'. Finally, however, a final draft was agreed by the UN Human Rights Council in June 2006 and this was then adopted by the UN General Assembly on 13 September 2007. Only four countries voted against the adoption of the Declaration: Australia, Canada, New Zealand and the US, all countries with significant indigenous minorities. All four have since formally endorsed the Declaration, though noting some reservations: Australia in 2009, and the three others in 2010.

The adoption of the Declaration was a landmark achievement, clearly articulating not only the rights of indigenous individuals and peoples but also the responsibilities of the nation states in which they live. UN Secretary-General Ban Ki-moon said it was a 'historic moment when UN Member States and indigenous peoples have reconciled with their painful histories and are resolved to move forward together on the path of human rights, justice and development for all'.

Ways of living

Indigenous peoples can be distinguished according to their different ways of life – how they survive and produce. These days, many have left their traditional life behind for the towns and cities, or work for wages part of the time and return to the land at other times of year. But the following descriptions still apply to hundreds of thousands of indigenous peoples worldwide, whether full- or part-time. People often practice mixed livelihoods; someone may be a pastoralist as well as a hunter-gatherer and cultivator, and earn cash in other ways too. But in most cases, the so-called subsistence economy is still the bedrock of how indigenous peoples make their living. These ways of living allow people to survive in very tough environments, wasting little or nothing, and are highly sustainable so long as there is enough space in which to move. That is changing as the industrial world encroaches upon indigenous peoples' fragile habitats.

Pastoralism

(15)

This pattern of life centers around animals, including cows, sheep, goats, reindeer, camels, yaks, horses, buffalo, llamas and alpacas. Pastoralists depend on the products of their livestock for food, clothing, implements, oil, shelter materials, barter and trade. Livestock are also a mobile form of wealth, medium of exchange and symbol of close relationships. They are used to pay bridewealth. Some people see their animals as sacred, certainly god-given. Many pastoralists are nomadic or semi-nomadic, moving seasonally between highland and lowland pastures in search of grass, water and salt-licks. They also move to escape ticks and tsetse flies that cause fatal stock diseases, or to get away from wild game such as wildebeest that infect cattle with a disease called malignant catarrhal fever. By moving seasonally, stock-keepers allow pastures to regenerate. Land, water and other resources in a particular area are shared communally. It is now widely recognized that pastoralism is a sustainable way of using certain types of fragile ecosystems, such as arid lands and difficult mountain areas.

Hunting and gathering

People hunt animals and birds for food, and by-products such as fur, skin and feathers that can be made into clothing and household goods. As well as hunting, fishing and trapping, they also collect edible insects, grubs, fungi and plants such as roots, fruits, berries and nuts. All these items can also be sold or bartered. Besides food, these resources also provide medicines, stimulants, pesticides, poisons, bedding and building materials. Fibers can be woven into baskets and mats. Forest-dwelling people also gather honey; many see this as the most prized food in the forest. People like the Inuit of Alaska and Greenland fish all year round, but hunt other animals seasonally: seals and nesting birds in the spring, other sea mammals such as walrus over the summer and caribou in the autumn.

Some hunter-gatherers, such as the 'Pygmy' peoples of Central Africa (best referred to by the name of their particular group), are called 'immediate return' societies. That means they focus on the present, people get an immediate return for their labor, and most food is consumed the same day as it is gathered. The opposite are 'delayed return' societies in which work is spread out over many months and there is no immediate yield. (Capitalist Western society is the ultimate example of this, but

'As nomads we traveled constantly, never staying in one place for more than three or four weeks. This constant movement was driven by the need to care for our animals... seeking food and water to keep them alive.'

Waris Dirie, Somali, East Africa.

agricultural and pastoralist systems also broadly follow this pattern.) Hunting and gathering people usually live in non-hierarchical societies, which emphasize sharing and equality.

Subsistence agriculture

This includes peasant farmers and shifting cultivators, who often complement their agriculture with hunting, fishing and the collection of wild foods. Subsistence farmers cultivate on a small scale, often on tiny plots of land, and may produce enough to feed their families but have little or no surplus to sell. Increasingly, subsistence farmers are forced to earn a living as day laborers on commercial farms or as seasonal migrant workers. Examples of indigenous peasant farmers include the upland Quechua people of Ecuador and the Aymara of Bolivia.

Shifting cultivation, sometimes also called 'slash and burn', is a type of agriculture followed by indigenous peoples in the tropical regions of Central Asia and lowland South America. Whole villages may move often, relieving the pressure on a piece of land. For example, the Kayapo people in the Brazilian rainforests plant out gardens in forest clearings and also hunt, gather and fish. The range and number of crops they grow help to offset any failures. The Karen of Burma grow rice in a seven-year cycle. They clear trees, burn vegetation, plant and harvest, moving to a new site every year, before returning to the original site after seven. This allows the forest and thin soils to recover before they start planting again.

Naga people in India and Burma also combine slash and burn with tilling more permanent irrigated rice terraces, making the most of their steep hilly terrain.

For reasons of space and practicality, this

> 'Men do the sowing and women, singing choruses and working with tiny hoes in a line behind, cover the grain with earth. This system also provides an opportunity for romance.'
>
> *Nagas*, see angelfire.com/mo/Nagaland/culture.html

Who are indigenous peoples?

> 'Every living animal that roams the country and every edible root that grows in the ground is common property.'
>
> *Yagan, an Australian Aboriginal man, in 1843.*

No-Nonsense Guide does not cover every indigenous society in the world. For example, it does not say much about the Roma, partly because they do not appear to self-identify as indigenous, and are not recognized as indigenous by the UN – (although they are seen as indigenous by the Center for World Indigenous Studies and there is an argument for including them).[8] But the book tries to give a broad overview, with as many representative examples as possible from different cultures, quoting indigenous people directly where possible. Many of the issues are contentious, so readers (including indigenous peoples) may not agree with everything.

The next chapter looks at what happened when explorers and colonizers first came across indigenous peoples. It was called 'discovery' – though of course, these people were there all the time. All 'discovery' meant was that Europeans found something and somebody new to them when they set sail to explore the outside world.

1 For more information, see Roxanne Dunbar Ortiz, *Indians of the Americas: Human rights and self-determination* (Zed Books 1984). **2** From iwgia.org **3** ILO Convention No 169, Article 1. Viewable at unhchr.ch/html/menu3/b/62.htm **4** *'Some Reflections on the Minority/Indigenous People Dichotomy'*, viewable at cwis.org/fsdp/international/untrtst2.txt **5** From iwgia.org **6** Edited version of *Operational Directive on Indigenous Peoples, September 1991*, The World Bank Operational Manual, worldbank.org **7** *State of the World's Indigenous Peoples*, UNFPII, un.org/esa/socdev/unpfii/en/sowip.html **8** UN recognition, and self-identification, will also tend to determine which other ethnic groups are included here.

2 Colonialism and conquest

First contacts with the outside world. Explorers and colonizers were followed by missionaries, anthropologists and administrators – and a trail of disaster was left behind.

ALTHOUGH PREJUDICE AGAINST and oppression of indigenous peoples is as old as the hills, the rot really set in with colonialism. When the European powers began carving up the world between them, they paid little regard to the local people who got in their way. In many cases they set out to exploit or exterminate them. Colonialism had a particularly devastating effect on indigenous peoples, because they were marginalized anyway, and had little or no power to resist. What follows applies to many communities, but to indigenous peoples in particular.

'The Indian must be made to feel he is in the grasp of a superior.'
Massachusetts clergyman George E Ellis, 1882.

'Kill every buffalo you can. Every buffalo is an Indian gone.'
Colonel Rl Dodge, US Army, 1870.

'But our Young men seeing several very handsome Young girls they could not help feasting their Eyes with so agreeable a sight… the poor young Girls seemed a little afraid, but very soon after turned better acquainted.'
George Robertson, master of the Dolphin, Tahiti, 1766-68.

'The Masai [sic] are a decadent race who have survived through being brought under the protection of British rule… They remain primitive savages who have never evolved and… in all probability, never can evolve.'
Rupert Hemsted, Officer in Charge of the Maasai Reserve, Kenya, 1921.

'The inhabitants of New South Wales, both male and female, go without apparel… From a disagreeable practice they have of rubbing themselves with fish-oil, they smell so loathsome, that is it almost impossible to approach them without disgust.'
Mary Ann Parker, A Voyage Round the World, 1795.

Colonialism and conquest

New national boundaries were drawn up, which cut across ethnic lines and put false divisions between people of the same race and language group. New systems of government and foreign laws were imposed, though some colonizers preferred to rule through local chiefs in a system called indirect rule, which left some of these traditional structures virtually intact. Native rights to land were not usually recognized, and vast areas were snatched for white settlement in the belief that they were 'waste lands' or 'empty lands'. Resources like water, forests and minerals were also taken over by colonial authorities, the church, individual settlers, commercial companies and the state, leaving local people struggling to survive on the worst patches of land. The transfer of plant species from the empire to Europe began an ecological imperialism (involving the 'theft' and control of indigenous fauna and flora) that has continued to this day. 'Native' reserves were created, corralling people in a kind of human cage where it was easier to control and tax them. Pastoralists were forced into reserves that stopped them moving seasonally in search of grazing and water. Then they were blamed for overgrazing and overstocking; they could not win.

In some countries, such as the US, Canada and Australia, aggressive attempts were made to assimilate indigenous peoples into the dominant society. Children were forcibly taken from their parents and sent either to white foster homes and adoptive parents or government-run boarding schools. The aim was to wipe out their culture, and make them act like whites. Children were beaten for speaking their own language, forced to wear European clothes and taught that European culture was superior. The result was a lost generation that developed a distorted image of themselves, low self-esteem and a great sense of loss. Indigenous peoples are still living with the legacy of what has been called 'acculturation as a weapon of war'.

First contact

First contact often spelled death for indigenous and other local peoples, especially if they did not submit to the whites. Exploration began in earnest from the 15th century onwards, when explorers set sail from Europe in search of riches, the source of the Nile (something that had long fascinated travelers to Africa), new territories and discoveries of all kinds.

Robinson Crusoe, Daniel Defoe's 1791 novel, has been called 'a blueprint for the British colony: nature tamed, the undergrowth cleared or made productive; the natives either faithful, trained servants like Man Friday, or dead, mowed down by disciplined soldiers with guns'.[1] The same could be said of explorers and colonizers from other nations. Brutality, theft of land and enslavement were three common hallmarks of first contact, though there were individual exceptions of Europeans who sided with native peoples and appreciated their rich culture. Here is how the Pende people of the Congo saw the Portuguese, as told by Pende oral historian Mukonzo Kioko:

'Our fathers were living comfortably... They had cattle and crops; they had salt marshes and banana trees. Suddenly they saw a big boat rising out of the great ocean. This boat had wings all of white, sparkling like knives. White men came out of the water and spoke words that no-one understood. Our ancestors took fright; they said these were vumbi, spirits returned from the dead. They pushed them back into the ocean with volleys of arrows. But the vumbi spat fire with a noise of thunder. Many men were killed... From that time to our days now, the whites have brought us nothing but wars and miseries.'[2]

In the US, the Spaniard adventurer De Soto made a habit of accepting the hospitality of friendly 'Indians' and then turning on them, killing and wounding people, kidnapping their leaders and burning crops and villages. His aim was to make indigenous peoples 'stand in terror of the Spaniards'. Fortunately for them he died in

1542, in what is now Arkansas. His cronies, fearing that the locals might take revenge, ran away. Relationships between some immigrants and indigenous races were initially warmer than this. Christopher Columbus (Cristóbal Colón), arriving in the Caribbean in 1492, told his royal patrons, the king and queen of Spain, that the local Arawak people were wonderfully generous and handsome. He claimed part of the Caribbean for Spain, was greeted as a dignitary and ally by the Taíno people and went home full of enthusiasm. But he saw the Taíno as potential serfs, telling his queen: 'They are fit to be ordered about and made to work.' The following year Colón returned to the region and founded the Spanish colony of Isabela on the island of Hispaniola. Gold was found, and indigenous people were enslaved to work in mines and plantations on their own land. They tried to resist and were brutally put down; the Spanish vowed that 100 Taíno would die for every European killed. By 1500 there were few Taíno left: three million of them had succumbed to massacres, famine, disease and slavery.

European immigrants to the US who are celebrated as heroes by mainstream society today included Ulysses S Grant who murdered Apaches, Andrew Jackson who killed Creek, Seminole and Cherokee people, and Thomas Jefferson who ordered the massacre of Shawnee and Kickapoo. Colonel John Washington, whose grandson became the first US president, executed Susquehannock leaders in Maryland in 1675; though tried for murder, he was not convicted. There are countless other examples from the New World.

What was happening elsewhere? German explorer Dr Carl Peters was notorious for the way he shot his way through East Africa in the 1890s. He believed in using bullets to show Africans who was boss, writing unashamedly of how he treated the Maasai: 'I have found... that the one thing which would make an impression on these wild sons of the steppe was a bullet from the repeater or the double-barreled rifle, and then only when employed in emphatic relation to their own bodies.'³

When Captain Cook landed in Australia in 1770, he had been ordered by the Crown not to take land without native consent, or unless it was uninhabited, but he went ahead and claimed the east coast in the king's name. When the first boat came ashore, Aboriginal people attacked the visitors with spears, and were driven back by bullets. The British did not settle until 1788, when they claimed Aboriginal land, saying it was empty and belonged to no one. But Aboriginal people had been there for 60,000 years, living in 600 to 700 clans, each with its own territory, political system and laws. The earliest settlers were convicts, many of them transported for petty crimes and anti-government politics. They were later joined by 'free' settlers, come to make their fortunes in the new colony. The convicts, their jailers and the free settlers may have been very different types of people. But the majority had one thing in common: scorn for Aboriginal people, which often manifested in horribly cruel acts including rape and murder.

The scientist Charles Darwin (1809-82) came across Aboriginal people in New South Wales in 1836. He could see at once what their fate was:

'The number of aborigines is rapidly decreasing... wherever the European has trod, death seems to purse the aboriginal. We may look to the wide extent of the Americas, Polynesia, The Cape of Good Hope and Australia, and find the same result... The varieties of man seem to act on each other in the same way as different species of animals – the stronger always extirpates the weaker. It was melancholy at New Zealand to hear the fine energetic natives saying that they knew the land was doomed to pass from their children.'⁴

Here he sounds sympathetic towards indigenous peoples. But Darwin's theories of evolution and natural selection were to have a massively harmful effect on relations between the so-called 'advanced' and aboriginal societies. The latter were said to be at a lower level of evolution, with smaller brains and less brainpower, and the unscrupulous and racists used this to justify slavery, apartheid, the Holocaust and colonial massacres. However, Darwin also wrote that the different races of humankind were descended from a common ancestor, and that there were many points of similarity between them.

Was first contact all bad?

In some places, there were limited benefits from first contact and first settlement. These included trade and employment, and some people happily intermarried, too. For a trade example, the captains and crews of early 16th-century French and English fishing vessels, working off Canada's Atlantic coast, traded furs with indigenous peoples. Later, beaver pelts were much in demand for hat making in Europe, and again it was the local inhabitants who supplied them. Champlain, who founded the first permanent white settlement in Canada at Quebec in 1608, traded with Algonkians and Hurons, hired them as guides, and gave them military help in fighting their enemies, the Iroquois. But the poisoned chalice was guns: Indians soon found that they were far superior to their own weapons, and bartered their valuable products for arms. They lost the art of making their own weapons, fought among themselves for monopoly of the fur trade, and became more desperate as over-hunting decimated the animals they had relied upon. Over time, their social system broke down as they moved from hunting for their own use in migratory bands to hunting for trade, which could be done more effectively in family groups.[5]

Making people sick

Colonialism also brought new diseases, which struck down indigenous peoples in their thousands. The killers included measles, influenza, smallpox, typhus, whooping cough, TB and venereal diseases, to which local people had no immunity. Some colonizers deliberately killed indigenous people by giving them smallpox-infected blankets – stories are still told about this today in Canada and the US. An unidentified disease, very probably spread from white settlements, killed off all the Native Americans on a long stretch of New England coast in the 1600s. On signing a treaty with the newcomers in 1621, Massasoit, chief of the Wampangoags, told them: 'Englishmen, take that land, for none is left to occupy it. The Great Spirit… has swept its people from the face of the earth.'

The Spanish conquistadores under Cortés were able to subdue the peoples of Mexico in 1520 when smallpox (which had probably arrived on one of their ships) took hold, killing tens of thousands. Famine followed, after unharvested crops were left rotting in the fields. The conquerors and their later apologists saw these diseases as divine retribution for 'savage' sins. One 17th-century author wrote about how Mexicans had been wiped out by 'vices, drunkenness, earthquakes, illnesses and recurring epidemics of smallpox and other diseases with which God in His mysterious wisdom has seen fit to reduce their numbers'. The silent killer then traveled to South America overland through the Maya kingdoms of Central America, Panama and over the Andes. It is said to have wiped out half the Incas, including the emperor Huayna Capac and his eldest son and heir.

Venereal disease was allegedly introduced to Australia by Europeans, though the settlers called it 'black pox' and blamed Aboriginal people for infecting them. Settlers frequently shot dead Aboriginal women they suspected of having given them the pox. Decadent sailors took the disease across the oceans; months at sea, when they were unable to get proper treatment, made their state all the worse by the time they arrived on land, desperate for sex with the nearest available women. Tahitians claim that explorer Louis De Bougainville's sailors first brought venereal disease to their island paradise in 1768.

All told, whether deliberate or accidental, some estimates put the numbers of people who died as a result of newly introduced diseases at 80 to 90 per cent of the original populations in North America, large parts of Central and South America, Australia and New Zealand/ Aotearoa.

Here are some examples of population slumps from disease and other factors linked to colonialism: Australian Aboriginals fell from at least one million pre-colonially to 30,000 by the 1930s; Maori from a quarter million to 42,000 by 1890; Polynesians on Tahiti from 40,000 in 1769 to 6,000 by the 1840s; 11 million indigenous Americans died in the 80 years after the Spanish invaded Mexico; Indians in Brazil fell from at least 2.5 million to 225,000 after Portuguese conquest (recent archeological evidence suggests that the pre-conquest population figure is probably much too low); more than 8 million Incas lost their lives in the Andes; the numbers of Native Americans north of Mexico fell from more than 8 million to 800,000 by the end of the 19th century. At least 11 million Africans were sent as slaves to the Americas, but millions more are believed to have died en route. Many were left to die before they embarked, or died as a result of activities linked to slavery.[6] In the Congo, Central Africa, the population was cut by at least half between 1880 and 1920.[7] Smallpox and sleeping sickness were spread by the mass population movements that came with colonialism. One European visitor described seeing a 15-foot boa constrictor feasting on the flesh of smallpox victims, and vultures so full they could not fly.

Working for Europeans could be the end of you, too. Slavery was obviously the most extreme example, but other types of labor were also forced. This book does not examine pre-20th century slavery, because it is difficult to separate the victims who were indigenous from those who were not. The Portuguese were exposed by the pioneering British journalist Henry Nevinson for running slave plantations on the islands of Saõ

Tomé and Príncipe off West Africa with what they called 'indentured laborers' shipped from the mainland, years after the abolition of slavery. These may well have included members of African communities who identify themselves as indigenous today. In 1915 the death rate on the islands was estimated at 100 per 1,000 laborers. Before roads and railways, human porters were used to transport goods all over Africa, and they died in their thousands from disease, malnutrition and over-work, not to mention being eaten by lions.

A little later, even when people supposedly gave their labor willingly, new taxes forced Africans (and people in other parts of the empire) into wage labor in order to raise the necessary cash. They were recruited and conscripted into armies and police forces, hired to build public works like roads and railways, and press-ganged into working on plantations where conditions were terrible. All this movement was fatal for many laborers. Workers often had to travel far from home, to unfamiliar climates where they died of cold or fever. Many more Africans succumbed to disease and malnutrition, after being forcibly conscripted into Kenya's Carrier Corps in World War One, than those who died in combat – a staggering one in four of all conscripts died. (The Carrier Corps supplied porters for British soldiers fighting the Germans in East Africa. A suburb of Kenya's capital city, Nairobi, is still called Kariokor today.)

The killing fields

The very worst abuses in colonial Africa probably took place in King Leopold's Congo. Up to ten million Africans, indigenous and otherwise, are said to have died in the course of the Belgian monarch's bid to rape central Africa for rubber and other riches, from 1885 onwards. The Welsh explorer and journalist Henry Morton Stanley (he claimed to be American, one of his many lies) had paved the way for Leopold some years before, by staking claims to the Congo on his behalf. Stanley –

wrongly hailed as a great hero, then and since – also did his share of killing Africans and burning villages. One member of his party stuck the severed head of an African in a box of salt and sent it to London to be stuffed and mounted by a taxidermist.[8] Under Leopold, the suffering continued on a massive scale. This was state-sponsored terror. People had their hands cut off for failing to supply enough rubber, and hands and feet were also cut off corpses to prove to officials how many Africans had been killed in a given area. Others were flogged or jailed for disobedience, while women and children were taken hostage until their villages had provided the set quota of rubber. Starvation struck villages which had lost their productive adults, or because they were forced to supply Leopold's soldiers with vegetables and fruit.

Some colonizers deliberately massacred indigenous peoples to get them out of the way, or by engineering tribal wars, encouraged one group to fight another and do their job for them. This is how the Governor of Louisiana congratulated himself on triggering a war between the Choctaw and Chickasaw peoples in the 17th century:

'The Choctaws... have raised about 400 scalps and make 100 prisoners... [This] is a most important advantage that we have obtained, the more so, that it has not cost one drop of French blood, through the care I took of opposing these barbarians to one another. Their self-destruction in this manner is the sole efficacious way of insuring tranquility in the colony.'[9]

In Tasmania, most of the Aboriginal inhabitants were either murdered or died of introduced disease between 1804 and 1834, and the remnants were put on an island in the Bass Strait between Tasmania and Australia where they literally pined away. The so-called laws of natural selection were used (here and elsewhere) to justify such murder as a duty. Rape was also commonly used as a weapon and demonstration of white male control. Stockmen on Tasmanian farms regularly kidnapped

Last of the Tasmanians

One of the last Tasmanian Aboriginal people was Truganini, daughter of a chief. She saw her mother stabbed to death by whites, her sister kidnapped and her uncle shot dead. Aged 15, she and her fiancé were taken by a couple of white men on a boat ride. The sailors threw her partner overboard. He could not swim and clung desperately to the boat. The white men chopped his hands off; after he drowned, they raped Truganini.

She later came to live on Flinders Island, where the last community of Tasmanian Aboriginals was confined. Even in death, she suffered humiliation. According to Aboriginal custom, she should have been cremated. Instead, her skeleton was put on show in Hobart Museum. In 1976, Truganini's remains were at last cremated and her ashes scattered in the sea. ■

Aboriginal women for sexual purposes. One of the most notorious episodes took place in 1827 at Cape Grim, when some white shepherds tried to take advantage of the local women. Their menfolk intervened, there was a fight and two people were wounded, one on each side. In revenge the Aboriginal men attacked the shepherds' flocks, and killed 118 sheep by spearing or throwing them over the cliffs. The shepherds had the last word. They killed at least 30 Aboriginals, throwing their bodies after the sheep.[10]

In some African colonies, soldiers were sent on so-called 'punitive expeditions' to suppress tribal revolts. In German East Africa the Germans hanged 12 Barabaig elders and their chief medicine man, Gidamowsa, leaving their bodies to rot on the scaffold as a warning to others. Often the warriors of one group were hired to attack their neighbors, and were 'paid' in loot such as raided cattle. Pastoralists who had lost thousands of stock in the rinderpest epidemics at the end of the 19th century were only too happy to help because they recouped their losses in this way. But some African populations slumped between 1880 and 1900 as a result of these raids and the starvation that followed them because farming was disrupted.

Colonialism and conquest

German colonizers brutally suppressed the Maji Maji rebellion in German East Africa in 1905-7 – the most serious challenge by Africans to colonial rule in this period. They also massacred Herero people in German South West Africa (now Namibia) between 1901 and 1906. The Herero revolted in 1904, killing 100 Germans, destroying some farms and raiding cattle. The response was far more vicious: between 75 and 80 per cent of the total Herero population of 60,000-80,000 were killed, women and girls were raped before being bayoneted, 14,000 people ended up in prison camps and 2,000 fled to South Africa. Soon after the Herero rose up, so did their neighbors the Nama. The Germans seized their land and livestock, so the Nama had no way of surviving. They were offered food and jobs if they gave themselves up. After their leaders Jacob Morenga – hailed as a kind of African Robin Hood – and Hendrik Witbooi were killed in battle, the Nama lost the will to fight on.

Bibles and labels

In the footsteps of the explorers came missionaries and later anthropologists. There is a much-repeated saying about how indigenous peoples lost their land, which crops up in different parts of the world with slightly different wording: 'With one hand you gave us the Bible, and with the other you took away our land.' In other words, we were distracted and duped. That is not quite true in every case – missionaries were by no means all bad, and they did not always have the power to take the land, though colonial rulers and governments did. On the positive side, missions offered education to non-whites at a time when the state did not. Education became the route out of oppression and poverty for many, and former mission pupils helped to liberate their countries from colonialism in the independence struggles of the 1950s and 1960s. Some early missionaries were quite radical and opposed government oppression of 'native' people.

Live human exhibits

In the age of high imperialism, from about 1850 to 1915, it became fashionable to put 'primitive' people on show at exhibitions. It was the age of Great Exhibitions, or World's Fairs as they were called in the US, and people flocked in their millions to see human freak shows presented as 'educational'. Photos of colonized peoples also became very popular, mostly taken by anthropologists and travelers. Many of these images, and the whole tone of such exhibitions, were racist. Their main message was that indigenous people were more primitive and backward than Europeans.

They did not just hurt the individuals who took part, physically and emotionally. They also helped to justify colonialism, and damaged the communities these people came from, many years after the event. They peddled ideas about racial difference and 'savagery' that are still current today. 'Bushmen' (San) were placed alongside baboons. Supposedly historical re-enactments of events like the Matabele War of 1893 showed Africans being defeated by white heroes. Non-whites, particularly women, were shown naked and eroticized to feed Western fantasies. At the US exhibitions, Native Americans were often shown in the most negative light.

Circus impresario Phineas T Barnum was behind many of these displays, which masqueraded as seriously anthropological. Barnum's Ethnological Congress in 1880 featured a human parade made up of misshapen, non-white bodies ('ugly' people, and so-called dwarves and giants) contrasted with those of 'perfect' white Americans. Barnum liked to describe his exhibits as savage cannibals who spoke no English. In fact, his three 'Fijian man-eaters' shown at the Philadelphia Exhibition in 1876 had been brought up on a Christian mission, were not cannibals, and spoke good English.

Ota Benga, a Mbuti 'Pygmy' from the Congo, was taken to the US as an object of curiosity. He appeared in the St Louis World's Fair of 1904, the New Orleans Mardi Gras and even at the Bronx Zoo. Later he lived in an orphans' home in Brooklyn, and attended a seminary in Virginia. Unable to take any more humiliation, he committed suicide in 1916.

Saartjie 'Sarah' Baartman was a Khoisan woman from the Eastern Cape In South Africa, a slave to Dutch farmers, who was transported to Britain in 1810 to be exhibited around the country to people who were fascinated by her physique - particularly her prominent buttocks. Known as 'the Hottentot Venus', she was later sold to a French animal trainer who exhibited her under even more pressurized and degrading conditions than In Britain. She died of an infection, probably smallpox, in 1815. After the liberation of South Africa, then-President Nelson Mandela petitioned France for the return of her remains and this finally happened In 2002. ∎

Colonialism and conquest

But most missionaries tended to scorn local customs, lifestyles, dress, language, religion and spirituality. Their main aim was 'improvement', on the assumption that indigenous and tribal peoples were at a low stage of human development. They railed against polygamy and tried to stamp it out, ignoring the fact that a man's 'spare' wives and children would be effectively thrown on the scrap heap and left to fend for themselves. They tried to force nomads to settle in one place, where they could be preached at more easily. They forced people into trousers, skirts and shoes. They tried to stop people speaking their own tongue, forcing children into schools where the main 'diet' – taught in a Western language – was religious dogma. (Later, the curriculum broadened to include more useful subjects; if lucky, you got a missionary who took a real interest in the advancement of his or her pupils.)

The earliest, self-styled anthropologists were often colonial administrators who studied local customs and languages as a hobby. They set about classifying the races of the new colonies. People were pigeon-holed according to how 'savage' they seemed, on a sliding scale from civilized to savage human being. Darwinism and the theory of natural selection were popular new ideas, and influenced how non-Western people were categorized. These classifications have stuck to people ever since – in Africa and other parts of the world today, some non-indigenous people still look down on indigenous peoples as a lower form of life.

Prejudice against nomads and hunter-gatherers

In the colonial period, many indigenous peoples were classified 'savage' and 'primitive' because they were not cultivators but pastoralists or hunter-gatherers. The idea that people who till the soil are more civilized than others is an ancient one, linked to the idea that settled people can make permanent improvements in their lives, both physical and intellectual.

Prejudice against nomads is very deep-seated. People who wander about have been dismissed for centuries as aimless, uncivilized, uncontrolled and therefore a threat to the state, greedy for more land than they actually need or use. In a 1937 study of nomads, anthropologist Ragnar Numelin wrote: 'The more primitive [man] is, the greater is his geographical influence and it then decreases to the degree in which he succeeds in becoming its master. In higher stages, the wandering need becomes materially modified.'[11] He called the cattle-keeping nomads of North Africa 'an army of loafers'. Nomads in general were 'cultureless peoples' with a 'psychological problem bound up in the wandering instinct'. It was a short step to saying nomads had small brains, and sure enough, he did.

Comparing the Maori favorably with other indigenous peoples who did not cultivate, the Archbishop of Dublin said they 'were very far from being in as low a state as the New Hollanders [Australian Aboriginals], for they cultivated the ground, raising crops of the cumera (a sweet potato), and clothed themselves, not with skins, but with mats woven by themselves'.[12] Lord John Russell, British Secretary of State for War and the Colonies from 1839-1841, also said approvingly that Maori people were 'not mere wanderers over an extended surface... in search of a precarious subsistence'.[13]

These ideas are very persistent. Roma and travelers have been dismissed for similar reasons, and equated with vagabonds and thieves. Hunter-gatherers do little better, often being described scornfully as backward forest people who must 'develop' if they want to be accepted by mainstream society. Today, whether indigenous peoples are still living in the old ways or not – keeping livestock or hunter-gathering, living in the city and working in an office – former prejudices remain. Old labels stick to new bottles, keeping indigenous peoples sidelined and 'justifying' bad treatment by governments, organizations and individuals.

Colonialism and conquest

The noble savage

There is a flip side to the coin that denounces indigenous peoples as savages, which is to exoticize them as 'noble savages'. This is just as bad in the end, because it still means that they and their rights are not taken seriously. They can end up like beautiful beasts in a human zoo, on display for everyone to stare at and photograph. Indigenous peoples who live in or near national parks and game reserves complain that this is how some tourists treat them – as an extension of the wilderness. The concept of wilderness is itself deeply problematic and ethnocentric.

The idea of the noble savage came from French philosopher Jean-Jacques Rousseau, writing in the 18th century. He believed that humans, in their original state, were beautiful, glorious and carefree; they only became corrupted and tainted by civilization. When the first travelers reached Tahiti (Wallis in 1767, Bougainville in 1768 and Cook in 1769), they saw it as an earthly paradise. European readers fell upon their journals in delight, believing that they confirmed Rousseau's ideas about the noble savage. The writer Diderot, a friend of Rousseau, reacted differently. When he read Bougainville's account of the Tahitians, he urged that they should be left alone. Addressing the Tahitians, he wrote: 'One day they [the Christians] will come, with crucifix in one hand and the dagger in the other to cut your throats or to force you to accept their customs and opinions; one day under their rule you will be almost as unhappy as they are.'

And the story goes on...

What colonialism and first contact began, the modern world has continued to do. At independence, power was handed over to local élites who pushed a nationalist agenda that was often unsympathetic to indigenous peoples. In many countries, these élites have hung on to power ever since, ruthlessly suppressing dissent. Giant industries, hydroelectric dams and mining operations have displaced thousands of indigenous peoples from their land. Their knowledge is 'ripped off' in the name of scientific advancement. Many are still seen as 'uncivilized', and the non-indigenous world looks down on them with contempt. The next chapter examines the problems facing indigenous peoples today, many of which stem directly from colonization and the attitudes it spawned, for imperialist attitudes helped to shape long-term policies towards indigenous peoples.

1 Felix Padel, 'Forest knowledge: tribal people, their environment and the structure of power', in *Nature and the Orient*, RH Grove, V Damodaran, S Sangwan (eds) (OUP 1998). 2 Adam Hochschild, *King Leopold's Ghost*, (Papermac 2000). 3 Carl Peters, *New Light on Dark Africa*, (Ward, Lock & Co 1891). 4 Charles Darwin, *Journal of Researches into the Natural History and Geology of the Countries visited during the Voyage of HMS Beagle Round the World*, 1839. 5 Adapted from *Canada's Indians*, MRG Report No 21 (1982). 6 Mark Cocker, *Rivers of Blood, Rivers of Gold: Europe's conflict with tribal peoples* (Pimlico 1999). 7 Hochschild, *Ghost*, quoting Jan Vansina. 8 Hochschild, *Ghost*. 9 From James Wilson, *The Original Americans: US Indians*, MRG Report (1986 edition). 10 Cocker, *Rivers of Blood*. 11 Ragnar Numelin, *The Wandering Spirit* (Macmillan 1937). 12 R Whately, *On the Origin of Civilisation* (London 1855). Cumera is kumara. 13 Russell to Hobson, 9 December 1840, CO 380/122, Public Records Office, London.

3 Land and nature

Why the earth is so vital for indigenous peoples, both practically and spiritually. Yet increasing numbers live in cities or are embracing private ownership, and we should beware the temptation to romanticize.

LAND IS LIFE ITSELF for many indigenous peoples. The lives of those who are not urbanized revolve around land and natural resources such as pasture, forest, honey, water, salt-licks, wildlife, domestic animals and wild plants that provide food and medicine. Unlike the majority of non-indigenous folk, they do not tend to see the natural world in terms of profit – it has deeper meaning, other kinds of value. However, that is changing as greed, cash and Western values such as individualism reach into every corner of the globe. What follows refers to many, but not all, indigenous peoples.

The natural environment is at the heart of their identity and culture. The human life cycle mirrors that of the natural world, and is believed to be circular rather than linear. One of the best examples of this is Australian Aboriginal beliefs about the Dreamtime. Aboriginal people relate totally to the earth, derive their spiritual power from it, and draw from the Dreamtime their ideas about how best to look after the environment. They believe the spirit of life exists for ever, and manifests itself in the landscape.

Knowledge of the environment

People who live largely by pastoralism, hunting, gathering or fishing have to know their environment intimately – they can almost read it like a book. They even come to know it as a kind of person with shifting moods; the relationship is a highly personal and emotional one. They must learn to manage the environment sensibly and sustainably or risk losing the bedrock of their lives and ecosystems.

Living on the land for generations, indigenous peoples

In the Dreamtime

Aboriginal people call the process of creating the world the Dreamtime, or in northern Queensland, the Storytime. They believe that the world was created by many male and female ancestors in the form of birds, animals, fish, insects, clouds, thunder, water, and also items made by people, like spears and dilly (string) bags. These beings came out of the earth, and made all the features of the landscape. Along the way, they often changed from human to animal, bird to plant, and other transformations. When they had done what they came to do, they went to ground again. There they stayed for evermore, in particular places, becoming a source of spiritual power. They are linked by stories or 'songlines' and nurtured by people acting out – through ritual and in their everyday activities – what the beings did in the Dreamtime. These actions mirror the myths and keep them alive. The landscape is believed to be animated by these beings. People often say their ancestral land is their mother or father, who has 'brought them up' and nourished them. Though the landscape is both male and female, women play a big part in the Aboriginal belief system. 'Spirit children' are believed to jump up into women's wombs at water sources or sacred sites, and this spirit presence is revealed through a sign appearing in the landscape. This may take the form of a bird or animal behaving in an unusual way, or appearing in an unexpected place. Such a place is believed to be the child's spiritual home, and he or she is considered responsible for that piece of land.

Every aspect of life is explored in the ancestral myths, and all the stories are very practical – they tell people how and where to hunt, gather food, cook, store things and make tools. Therefore myths combine practical knowledge with spiritual knowledge. When they die, people believe they return 'home' to be reunited with their totemic being, such as a bird, fish or wallaby. They must go back to a specific place; no other place will do.

'We come back la our own country again… when I die they gonna send my spirit back here, that's my home see, my land. I gotta come back here. We bin come from here, we gotta come back here. Same place.' ■

The quotation at the end comes from an interview with Winston Gilbert by Veronica Strang in Alaine Low and Soraya Tremayne, *Women as Sacred Custodians of the Earth? Women, spirituality and the environment* (Berghahn Books 2001).

come to know where and when to find honey, nutritious or medicinal wild plants, track down animals to kill and eat, find the best grazing, water sources and salt-licks, or catch the biggest fish. They know how to find and stitch certain leaves together to make cups, plates and other

Land and nature

household goods. They know that the twigs of some trees make excellent toothbrushes, certain leaves make natural deodorants, and the boiled bark of other trees is good for the digestion. A certain kind of grass makes good bedding, because the smell keeps biting bugs away. One herb cures coughs, another diarrhea. Tea made from a particular root cures fever. And if you want to get 'high', or mask the pain of illness or injury, there is always something natural you can take. Often such people live in very harsh environments, where anyone else would soon starve or die of illness, far from any modern hospital.

For example, by following the wisdom and traditions of their ancestors, the San people[1] of southern Africa were able to survive in very dry areas by gathering nutritious wild plants and by burying water in ostrich shells along the routes they traveled. Today, their lifestyle is changing as they have lost their land to game reserves and cattle herding, which has taken over large areas of their traditional territory. But those who still hunt use poisoned arrows – with poison made from natural substances – and cleverly track their prey for many miles until the wounded animal becomes drugged and falls down. They use every part of the animals they hunt, taking care not to hurt females and their young. To take the example of just one San group, the Ju | 'hoansi or !Kung (found in Namibia, Angola and Botswana) live off 55 different species of animal, eat more than 100 different species of wild plants and know exactly where to collect vegetables and fruits that ripen at different times of year.[2]

The Sanema people of Venezuela live in the rainforest. They move their farm plots often, practicing a low-impact form of agriculture that allows the soil to recover. The types of crops they plant – bananas, cassava, plantains and yams – take the minimum from the nitrogen-poor soil. They supplement their diet with meat and other forest produce, going into the forest to live temporarily and hunt with bows and arrows. The Tukano people of Brazil and Colombia practice sustainable fishing, striking a fine balance between their food needs, the needs of the fish and the wellbeing of the forest, too. The Tukano fish only certain areas of the Uaupes River; each community decides what part of river they will fish, leaving some stretches alone, which allows them to become spawning grounds. Cultivation and the felling of trees along river banks is banned, because it is believed that these areas belong to the fish. As Paulinho Paiakan, leader of the Kayapo people of Brazil, puts it: the rainforest is 'our university'.

Traditional ecological knowledge (TEK)

Traditional ecological knowledge now has a label – TEK. Some people also call it ethno-ecology. Western scientists increasingly recognize its value; they want to learn from it, and document it properly. Indigenous peoples are demanding the right to take part in this kind of study on their own terms. They are wary of having their knowledge stolen by Western drug companies, which have made a lot of money out of indigenous medicine. Many of the prescription medicines derived from plants, and now available globally, were only discovered through talking to indigenous peoples.

Now some indigenous groups are taking steps to patent plants, so that they can retain a measure of control over their scientific and medical uses. But other indigenous groups are not agreed that such attempts to patent plants are useful for protecting the traditional knowledge base. Still others feel that patents and the very idea of intellectual property are incompatible with traditional values built on communal rights and on oral knowledge being passed on through generations. It is a controversial area.

Land and nature

A good example of collaboration using TEK between scientists and indigenous peoples took place in New Zealand/Aotearoa. The Ngati koi people (a tribal group, or iwi in Maori) worked with researchers from the National Institute of Water and Atmospheric Research (NIWA) on the history of the Ohinemuri River, North Island. Together, they presented historical evidence of ecological damage, largely caused by gold-mining, in their claim to the Waitangi Tribunal, which is hearing Maori claims arising from the colonial Waitangi Treaty made between Maori chiefs and Britain. Science and traditional knowledge came together to record this history. Besides looking at old archives, the team also gathered oral evidence from Maori people. 'Our people have more than 80 years' experience of the river,' says Ngati koi spokesperson Joel Williams. 'They also have

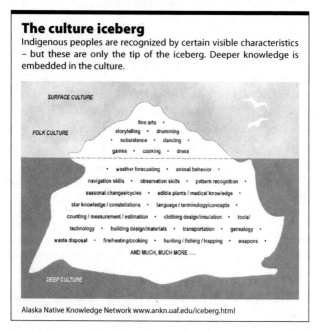

The culture iceberg

Indigenous peoples are recognized by certain visible characteristics – but these are only the tip of the iceberg. Deeper knowledge is embedded in the culture.

SURFACE CULTURE

FOLK CULTURE

fine arts
storytelling • drumming
• subsistence • dancing
games • cooking • dress

• weather forecasting • animal behavior •
navigation skills • observation skills • pattern recognition •
seasonal changes/cycles • edible plants / medical knowledge •
star knowledge / constellations • language / terminology/concepts •
counting / measurement / estimation • clothing design/insulation • tools/
technology • building design/materials • transportation • genealogy •
waste disposal • fire/heating/cooking • hunting / fishing / trapping • weapons •
AND MUCH, MUCH MORE . . .

DEEP CULTURE

Alaska Native Knowledge Network www.ankn.uaf.edu/iceberg.html

the recollections of their ancestors, who have resided along the river for over 12 generations.' The river used to be home to thriving quantities of whitebait, eel and fish, while the forest around it used to teem with birds. The biodiversity of the river is now much reduced.[3]

Bryce Cooper of NIWA explains what the Ngati koi were trying to prove: 'Their traditional uses of the river and its margins (for example, eels as a food source, flax for weaving) have been damaged by the activities of the European settlers – gold-mining, farming, sewage discharges. Also, in Maori tradition the status of an iwi or tribal group is built upon the good quality of the natural resources over which it has stewardship rights.'[4] The research concluded that the river and its surroundings had indeed been severely damaged. The scientists could not have proved this on their own, says Bryce Cooper. 'Ngati koi knowledge added much to the case as it provided a longer time scale of information than was possible from our science data, and supported our science inferences regarding the past character of the river and what fish populations could have been there prior to farming and gold-mining.'

Collective ownership

The idea that land can be privately owned was (and often still is) anathema to indigenous peoples, although moves towards privatization are changing attitudes and behavior. Indigenous groups traditionally saw land – and other resources like water, plants and wild animals – as something belonging to the whole community. You have to share it. You do not grab more than your fair share. You do not plunder everything in sight without putting something back. And you cannot buy and sell it, as Crowfoot, a Blackfoot Native American chief, tried to explain to white Americans:

'Our land is more valuable than your money. It will last forever... As long as the sun shines and the waters flow, this land will be here to give life to men and animals. We cannot

sell the lives of men and animals. It was put here for us by the Great Spirit and we cannot sell it because it does not belong to us. You can count your money and burn it within the nod of a buffalo's head, but only the Great Spirit can count the grains of sand and the blades of grass on the plains. As a present to you, we will give you anything we have that you can take with you; but the land, never.'[5]

The South American Incas made sure that everyone had access to land which was held by the *ayllu* – the community or kinship group. In the Western Ghats area of south India, indigenous peoples used a form of shifting cultivation called *kumri* that allowed them to manage communally-held land in an ecologically sound way. (The colonial British saw the cultivators as barbaric vagrants, and banned *kumri* because they said it threatened the forests.)[6] The whole basis of Native American society was co-operative, and that included the way people managed their environment. In colonial Africa, European powers took advantage of the fact that most ethnic groups did not 'own' land in the Western sense, and seized millions of hectares – calling it 'vacant' and 'wasteland'. But from the African savannas to the Australian outback and the North American plains, tribal and indigenous peoples saw land and the natural world as something to be shared. These attitudes began to change with colonialism. After Europeans began arriving and staking claims to land, some indigenous leaders realized that although they had legitimate customary rights to their lands, they had better stake a European-style legal claim, too, or see it all disappear. Hence some went to court or registered land titles in an attempt to defend what was theirs in the first place. To this day, indigenous peoples are demanding recognition of their ownership of traditional lands, not simply their rights to use and occupy it.

In recent years there has, however, been an increasing trend towards private ownership of what was formerly indigenous land. In October 2010, for example, the

Nisga'a people of northern British Columbia, Canada, passed a law allowing for private ownership on parts of their territory. Until that point all aboriginal reserve lands had for 130 years been under the ownership and protection of the federal government. But individuals – whether native or not – are now able to buy and sell property, including homes, on the land of the Nisga'a nation.

The Nisga'a leaders hope that this will unlock a prosperity that has hitherto been denied their people. Nisga'a President Mitchell Stevens said it would transform the 6,000-strong people's fortunes. Former chief of the Kamloops people Manny Jules agrees. Back in 1988, Jules won the right for native groups to collect taxes from commercial operations on reserve land. Now he argues that the inability of native people to own homes or raise mortgages within the reserves is holding back their entrepreneurial potential and stopping them overcoming their poverty and social problems.

Most indigenous leaders, however, remain opposed to the idea, seeing it as just another way in which they will lose access to their own land, which is at the heart of their collective identity. They point out that when reserve lands in the US were opened up to private ownership in 1887, many reserves were broken into pieces as non-native people bought parcels of land

This kind of dispute is being repeated in indigenous communities all over the world.

Spirit realms

Traditionally, indigenous people do not see land and nature as separate from the rest of life. The spiritual, the social and the material are all entwined, and everything is believed to connect with everything else. That makes indigenous people literally feel more grounded than people who have lost their roots, often in the concrete jungle – though, of course, increasing numbers of indigenous people, or those with indigenous roots, now find themselves in precisely those concrete jungles.

The environment is regarded as a sacred realm. God or gods are not generally believed to take a human form, as they do in, say, Christianity or Hinduism, but inhabit the natural world itself. God is thought to be all around, living in the landscape, and the earth is revered like a parent. Native Americans, for example, believe in a cosmic unity that embraces human beings, animals, plants and everything else. Humans must live in harmony with the whole or suffer the consequences. Shamans mediate between people and spirit beings in the landscape by performing various rituals, but ordinary people must also show respect for the spirits by obeying strict rules about hunting, eating and other activities. Before whites arrived and the economy began to change, the very existence of the Inuit people of Canada, Greenland and Alaska depended on being able to interpret the environment. They also believed it was inhabited by spirits, both good and bad, who could be influenced through shamans (see chapter 6).

> 'Land is my backbone. I only stand straight, happy and proud and unashamed of my color because I still have land.'
>
> *Aboriginal man, Australia*

Siberian reindeer herders, the Evén people, believe you must not whistle, sing or make a noise when out in the wilds because this might offend the spirits who own the forest. To be a successful hunter you must also respect the moods of animals and behave in a quiet, unobtrusive way. It is all about showing respect – even if you kill something. Damara herders of Namibia also believe one must stay silent when gathering wild foods out of respect for the ancestors, whose help is needed to collect them. They also guarantee people's safe passage through ancestral land. The Naga people of Asia believe both in a supreme god – a creator who is rather remote – and in earth spirits which have different functions. One is believed to be the goddess of crops and wealth, another the one who presides over all wild animals, and so on.

According to the Maori creation story, in the beginning was Te Kore or total darkness. There was no life, just potential. The Earth Mother, Papatuanuku, and the Sky Father, Ranginui, were locked in an embrace that shut out all light and prevented anything growing. Their children desperately wanted light, so they separated their parents by force. One of the sons, Tane Mahuta or God of the Forests, got between earth and sky. He pushed up as hard as he could with his legs until his father was prised apart from the earth. The God of the Winds, God of the Sea and all living things poured into the light that was created. Tane Mahuta made the first human being from the clay of his mother. He slept with her and made a daughter, Hinetitama. With Hinetitama, Tane conceived other children. When Hinetitama found out that her father and lover were the same person, she ran away to the underworld, where she still lives.

Earth mothers: women and the natural world

Women are often regarded, in indigenous and other communities, as sacred custodians of the earth. They give birth to new life, tend the earth and harvest its fruits, protect and nurture, and often play a central part in rituals to do with fertility, making rain, blessing earth, animals and crops. Spirit mediums are often women, who communicate between the spirit world, the environment and human beings. But some anthropologists and feminists argue that bracketing women with 'nature' brackets men with 'culture' and therefore places men in a more powerful and superior position – because culture is associated with reason and civilization, nature with something lower and wilder.

Either way, rural indigenous women tend to live very close to the natural world. Before hospitals arrived, and even afterwards, the women's task was to find and gather medicinal plants and cure the sick. Women and children collect the wild foods that form an important part of the diet. They make clothing and other items out of natural

Land and nature

materials, both for use at home and to sell or barter. They teach children about the environment and spiritual values.

Chiefs used princesses to perform 'eco-rituals' in old Zimbabwe. One of them, Muredzwa, was so famous as a rainmaker in the 19th century that rain was said to fall into her footsteps as she walked by. This ancient institution of princesses, whose jobs included enforcing 'traditional ecological laws', has recently been revived. They have tried to stop sacred groves being cut down, told men off for fencing pools that the whole community should be able to use, and banned the sale of caterpillars and locusts which they think god gave people to eat, not to sell.[7] At the same time, in Zimbabwe and other parts of the world, certain women have long been seen as a negative and dangerous force environmentally. An age-old fear in many cultures is that female witches blight crops, stop the rains coming and make animals fall sick.

Once were warriors

Urbanized indigenous people also retain a special link to the land. Though thousands of indigenous people no longer live in the countryside but in towns and cities, they are a significant part of the story. Most still feel deeply about the land, although they no longer live close to it. Some urban groups are now spearheading calls for indigenous land rights; they may be better placed than rural people to take on governments, corporations and lawyers. But this can lead to rivalry and jealousy, as more educated urban people speak on behalf of the silent majority. Some accuse urbanized people of getting an unfair slice of the cake, and doing this for personal glory, because they are closer to the seat of power – and may even be powerful politicians themselves. Conversely, urban people (and those of mixed ancestry) may have difficulty proving their rural roots and hence their territorial and other rights under treaties.

Back on the land, things are also changing. Privatization has increased, and with it monetization – many traditional resources and goods have a price now, preferably in cash. More and more people are embracing Western-style individualism. Exploitation of land and resources by transnationals is not only 'raping' those resources but also changing local people's values and way of life, as the next chapter will describe. Now that people realize the worth of land title, land in certain regions is being chopped up into smaller privately owned parcels, which are often too small to yield much. It has to be said that richer individuals, some of them indigenous and usually male, are themselves exploiting other indigenous people in this race to claim and carve up land. In some places, traditional ideas about sharing resources communally are being lost.

Beware too much romanticism...

Reverence for nature should not be confused with ecological soundness in all cases. Aboriginal peoples were not necessarily the world's first ecologists, as some people claim. Western awe of non-Western societies that live 'close to nature' can obscure the fact that some indigenous peoples' practices are not necessarily ecologically sound or sustainable. Or if they are, that came as a result of trial and error over many centuries. This awe can say more about Westerners themselves, disgusted by environmental destruction in their own backyard, looking eagerly to other societies to find something 'pure' and unspoiled. There is a need to be wary of blind reverence. It links to a long tradition in Western thought, which saw pre-colonial societies as

Land and nature

living in harmony and balance with nature – always 'living lightly upon the land', almost childlike in their ways. That is patronizing and too simplistic. Indigenous peoples were and are just as capable as anyone else of manipulating the natural world to suit themselves, and there is evidence, for example, of fauna and flora disappearing over time as a result of over-hunting and over-burning of vegetation.

Control over land is power in its purest and most basic form because it involves control over food, and therefore the means of survival. What is the fate of indigenous peoples who have lost their land, forests and other natural resources? One old man, a Batwa 'Pygmy' from the Great Lakes region of Central Africa, put it bluntly: 'Since we were expelled from our lands, death is following us. We bury people nearly every day. We are heading towards extinction.'[8] The next chapter will explore these crises and related problems in more detail.

1 The San do not have one name to describe themselves collectively. They are made up of 13 or more groups. But they prefer to be called San rather than the other names they have been given, such as Bushmen. They live in Botswana, Namibia, Angola, South Africa, Zimbabwe and Zambia. **2** Megan Biesele and Kxao Royal/O/oo, *San* (Rosen Publishing Group 1997). **3** *Aniwaniwa* online, Issue 17, niwa.cri.nz/pubs/an/17/science.htm **4** Personal communication, April 2002. **5** Miller, *From the Heart.* 19th century, no exact date given. However, this kind of statement has been exploited by governments who use it to claim that indigenous peoples had no traditional concept of land ownership prior to colonial contact. **6** Subash Chandran, 'Shifting Cultivation, Sacred Groves and Conflicts in Colonial Forest Policy in the Western Ghats' in Grove, Damodaran, Sangwan (eds) *Nature.* **7** From Terence Ranger, 'Priestesses and environment in Zimbabwe' in Low and Tremayne, *Women as Sacred Custodians.* **8** Unnamed man from Kalehe, DRC, quoted in Jerome Lewis, *The Batwa Pygmies of the Great Lakes Region*, MRG Report (2000).

4 Facing the problems

Indigenous peoples are under threat from all sides. Mining, logging and oil companies menace their land, as do commercial farmers. They may find themselves victims of conflict or victimized by security forces. They are more vulnerable to disease and suicide, and die younger than the general population. Overall, they lack the respect they deserve.

LOSS IS THE WORD that links many of the problems facing indigenous peoples today. Land loss is the most crucial, for without land there is no viable life and livelihood. Given the links between environment and identity, discussed in the last chapter, land loss also undermines cultural identity and wellbeing in a very fundamental way, and this explains why the land-rights issue is central to almost every declaration by indigenous peoples. After being torn from their lands, other losses are never far behind, including loss of resources, customary foods and plant medicines, extended family, language, freedom to roam, and the freedom to practice their own customs and religious rites in a place of their choosing. Forced urbanization has brought countless problems.

Indigenous peoples are among the most disadvantaged and discriminated against human beings in the world. They are often the poorest, with the worst health, housing, schooling and job opportunities. They suffer high rates of depression and other mental-health problems, suicide and substance abuse. Sometimes they are denied access to health services, welfare and schooling altogether. Where state schooling is offered, it may be used by governments as a tool for assimilation – in a bid to replace indigenous languages and culture with dominant, national ones.

In some cultures, indigenous women are in a subordinate position and enjoy few rights, though the bigger threat usually comes from national society. They

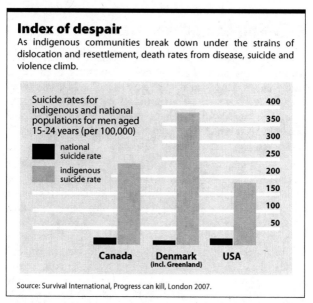

Index of despair

As indigenous communities break down under the strains of dislocation and resettlement, death rates from disease, suicide and violence climb.

Suicide rates for indigenous and national populations for men aged 15-24 years (per 100,000)

■ national suicide rate

■ indigenous suicide rate

Canada

Denmark (incl. Greenland)

USA

400
350
300
250
200
150
100
50

Source: Survival International, Progress can kill, London 2007.

are vulnerable to rape and sexual exploitation, especially by soldiers, police, employers and other powerful males. There have been shocking exposés of the high rates of black deaths in custody (such as those in Australia since 1980) – the result of police brutality, but passed off as suicide and 'misadventure' – and murders by police and the military in places like Colombia. Many of the victims are indigenous community leaders, targeted purely because of their efforts to achieve land and other collective rights (see chapter 5). It is also no accident that many 'down and outs', living on city streets in wealthy countries such as Canada, the US and Australia, have indigenous ancestry. Despairing and destitute, they have dropped off the map of the rich world.

Exploitation of land

Many of the indigenous peoples who survived into the 20th century did so because they lived in areas that once had no value for others. But companies now roam the globe looking for new resources to exploit. States, also driven by the profit motive, are eager to exploit resources they once saw as marginal and uneconomic. Expanding populations, the discovery of minerals and oil, the growth of modern communications and other factors have now ended the isolation of even the most remote indigenous groups. Indigenous lands are threatened by agriculture, roads, dams, irrigation projects, mines, oil extraction and timber logging. There are also many cases of pastoralists being evicted from their grazing lands to make way for wildlife parks. These are suddenly declared 'conservation areas' in which humans are said to have no place – which ignores the fact that pastoralists have often happily coexisted with wildlife for centuries, and helped to conserve and shape the very environment that is so prized by Western-dominated 'conservation' bodies. The same is true of hunter-gatherers and most shifting cultivators, too.

These activities are often linked to national development projects that ignore the welfare of indigenous peoples. Their resources are being taken without compensation.

Eat poison

Those who enter indigenous territory rarely take care of it – or its peoples.

● In Malaysia, the Penan people of Sarawak have had their rivers polluted with chemicals used by large-scale loggers, oil, rubbish and silt.

● In Peru, oil extraction in the Amazonian department of Loreto has led to contamination of water, fish and plants with heavy metals such as lead and cadmium. High levels are found in the blood of indigenous children.

● Amazonian people such as the Enawene Nawe, Ikpeng and Mehinako report contamination of the fish they eat by the agrochemicals from neighboring soy plantations and cattle ranches.

● High levels of PCBs and heavy metals have been found in the meat of marine species eaten by indigenous people in the Arctic.

Source: Survival International, Progress can kill, London 2007.

Facing the problems

When they resist, they feel the full force of state repression. They are blamed for being backward, for not embracing modernity. But why should they embrace 'development' that has been designed by and for others?

This said, a growing number of indigenous peoples around the world have negotiated with mining or other companies wishing to work on their land. Some groups are in favor of commercial exploitation of their land provided they either retain control or derive substantial monetary benefits. In Nunavut, Canada, for example, new diamond and gold mines have been opened since the establishment of the new province under indigenous control in 1999. In Australia, meanwhile, there are numerous such deals, among them the Midwest Gas Pipeline agreement of 1999, reached between a company and three native title groups in Western Australia and covering compensation payments and protection of heritage sites.

Nevertheless, there are all too many negative examples of indigenous peoples whose interests and well-being have been damaged by development.

Example 1: the Barabaig, Tanzania, East Africa

'This was prime grazing land. We can ill afford to lose such a large area of pasture.'[1]

Barabaig pastoralists lost a vast area of their most productive pastures to a Canadian aid-funded wheat scheme from 1970 onwards. Their government did not stop this; on the contrary, it signed up to the Tanzania Canada Wheat Program and handed over 100,000 acres to the National Agriculture and Food Corporation, to grow wheat by Canadian prairie-style mechanized methods. The wheat farms took over more than 12 per cent of Hanang District, where the Barabaig live, but the loss was much more than the size of land involved. It encroached upon a type of pasture they call *muhajega*, made up of nine very important species of grass and herbs. After the wheat farms came, and through other types of encroachment, the Barabaig lost virtually all their *muhajega*. They have been forced to over-rely on other kinds of pasture. Grazing that was once rested seasonally has been used more intensively, pastures are deteriorating and the herds do not produce as much as they did. Other environmental impacts include soil loss, bush clearance and gully erosion.

But there have been some positive outcomes. The Barabaig people launched an international campaign to defend their rights, and a legal challenge. A High Court judge ruled that they did have communal rights to the land, and that the wheat growers had trespassed, but no land was actually returned to them.

Since then a human rights commission and legal rulings have vindicated Barabaig claims, but there has been minimal compensation.

In 2005 a report of the UN Working Group of Experts on Indigenous Populations/Communities found that Barabaig displacement has continued to various parts of Tanzania and Malawi, with other communities routinely objecting to their presence. Although the project that displaced the Barabaig in the first place has since been abandoned, the land remains in the hands of the government, with talk of it being sold to willing buyers.

Example 2: the Yanomami, Brazil

'This is what we want – to live in peace. We are tired of death, of murders, of the destruction of the forest.' *Davi Kopenawa, Yanomami spokesperson*

The Yanomami are rainforest people, living deep in the Amazon straddling the border between Brazil and Venezuela. They had little contact with the outside world before the 1980s, when a gold rush prompted thousands of miners to invade their territory. This exposed them to killer diseases to which they were not immune, and to violence from miners and other settlers. One fifth of Yanomami were killed by disease and violence in just seven years during the 1990s. The roar of supply planes and the constant noise of generators and pumps used in mining scared away many of the game animals they hunted. High-pressure hoses washed away river banks, silting up the rivers and destroying spawning grounds. Mercury, used to separate gold from soil and rock, has been dumped in the rivers and poisoned people's food and water. The influx of miners has caused social upheaval that has led to a rash of begging, prostitution and drunkenness.

The Yanomami campaigned for their lands to be declared a reserve and the Brazilian government finally created a special territory in 1992.

Since then the Yanomami have set up their own health, education and bee-keeping projects, which have improved their situation. But this has not stopped the invasions. There was a massacre of 16 Yanomami

---

Impoverishment

Traditionally, indigenous people have tended to live simple but sustainable lives. A combination of colonialism, exploitation, racism and disastrous 'development policies' has made them poor. Prejudice severely restricts education and employment prospects, compounding poverty.

• Although they account for less than 5% of the global population, indigenous people comprise about 15% of all the poor people in the world.

• Average incomes of Australia's Aboriginal population are only 62% of those of the non-indigenous population.

• Ethnic-minority groups make up less than 9% of China's total population but are believed to account for about 40% of the country's extremely poor people.

• In India, 25% of the population live below the poverty line but among indigenous people the figure rises to 45%.

• In Thailand, more than 40% of indigenous girls who migrate to cities work in the sex trade.

• Living conditions on Canadian First Nations reserves were at the same level as those in a country ranked 78th in the UN Human Development Index at a time when Canada as a whole ranked 4th.

Source: *New Internationalist* 410, April 2008

by miners at Haximu in 1993. The illegal mining continues, and is thought to be at its most active in areas inhabited by Yanomami groups that have hitherto been uncontacted by 'civilization'.[2]

Conflict

Indigenous peoples are right in the firing line in conflicts around the world. In some cases, that is because their leaders have defied oppressive national governments and stood up for people's rights to self-determination. Indigenous peoples often happen to live in buffer zones between different nations and power groups who are at war. Sometimes they live in areas with rich resources coveted by transnational corporations, and war is being fought over rights to these resources.

Example 3: the Karamojong, Uganda

The Karamojong pastoralists of northeastern Uganda are a long way from Washington. But the 'New World Order' is impacting on them in surprising ways, as the post-September 11 anti-terrorism campaign leads to repressive measures against African pastoralists who need guns to ward off cattle raiders, just as many US citizens carry them for self-defense.

The 'warriors against terrorism' are now keen to support 'failing' states against any group of people who prefer to regulate themselves and who reject mainstream values. The 'New World Order' simply does not tolerate diversity. There is evidence that Washington was behind Ugandan government efforts to disarm the Karamojong forcibly, as if they threaten to destabilize the 'civilized world'.

When cultural resistance involves modern firearms, a small ethnic group can easily be seen as a threat to world security. There was a flood of weapons into this area after Idi Amin's troops fled the local barracks in 1979, leaving a full arsenal of AK-47s. The idea is that, by removing the guns, this corner of Uganda will return to normal, and world leaders will sleep more soundly in their beds – for one more state will have been saved from failing. But there is no evidence that any international terrorists are being harbored here, or that the Karamojong are a threat to anyone besides their immediate neighbors.

The forced disarmament program was strongly condemned in a 2006 report by the UN Office of the High Commissioner for Human Rights (OHCHR). Among the severe human rights violations it documented on the part of the national army, the Ugandan People's Defence Forces, were: extra-judicial killings of civilians, torture, inhuman and degrading treatment, the rape of a woman, and the widespread destruction of homesteads.

OHCHR's follow-up report in November 2007 noted a significant improvement in the security and human rights situation but it still demanded that those responsible for the abuses were brought to account and condemned the culture of impunity in the Ugandan armed forces.[3]

Crime, punishment and terror

Indigenous people are being criminalized in many ways. Increasingly they are being targeted using post-9/11 anti-terrorism laws.

• Chile's anti-terrorist laws have been used to give harsh 10-year sentences to Mapuche activists for a supposed 'terrorist' arson attack on a forestry plantation on disputed land.

• In Malaysia, Penan leader Kelesau Naan, an outspoken critic of logging companies, disappeared while out on a hunting trip in late 2007.

• In Brazil, at least 76 indigenous people were murdered in 2007 – an increase of 63% on the previous year.

• In the Philippines, at least 26 indigenous rights activists were killed in 2006 by security forces, apparently in an extra-judicial move to suppress protest against the president.

• In Oaxaca, Mexico, police clashed violently with indigenous people in 2006, leaving 17 dead and hundreds missing or wounded.

• In Australia, Aboriginal people are 15 times more likely than the general population to be imprisoned.

• In the Indian state of Orissa, 14 Adivasi people were killed in 2006 while protesting against a large steel plant on their land.

Source: *New Internationalist* 410, April 2008

Example 4: the Montagnards of Vietnam

The 53 indigenous ethnic minorities of Vietnam have had a long history of struggle with central government, from French colonialists to the communist state. They have suffered land losses and also been 'used' by both sides in conflicts, including the Vietnam War, when US Special Forces organized ethnic minority highlanders known collectively as Montagnards (from the French term 'mountain dwellers') into defense groups to prevent communist infiltration from the north. Though the rights of ethnic minorities are now enshrined in the Vietnamese constitution, their situation remains uneasy. Politicized highlanders today increasingly refer to themselves as Dega. Below, a man from Dak Lak, interviewed in July 2001, tells the story of the struggle...

'Since god gave birth to the world, we ethnic minorities have always been in the same place. Since antiquity, our ancestors have always told us that this is our land. The Vietnamese never lived here. What we learned from our grandparents is that Vietnam started invading our land in 1930... From the time the French left in 1954, the Vietnamese increased their presence until they were all over the place. In 1958, because the Vietnamese were getting stronger and stronger in the Central Highlands, all the ethnic minorities – Ede, Koho, Jarai, Stieng and Bahnar – stood up to make the first demonstration. All the ethnic minorities had one idea: we wanted our land back. The Vietnamese promised to give us our land back so there would be no more conflicts. They were not speaking the truth. Instead, they put our leader, Y Bham Enuol, in jail in Hue for seven years.

'In 1965 when they let Y Bham out of jail, the ethnic minorities started the FULRO movement. It was based in Cambodia. I was 12 years old and carried a gun that was as long as me. Everyone, young and old, joined the struggle. Later, in 1969, Nguyen Van Thieu, the president of South Vietnam, promised in the '033' agreement to give us our land back. Y Bham would be in charge of the Central

Facing the problems

Highlands and the Vietnamese would go back to Vietnam. Instead, Vietnam received foreign aid and used the Dega to fight against North Vietnam. Thousands of us were killed. In 1975, the [North] Vietnamese put our leader Nay Luett in prison for ten years. Vietnamese from both the north and the south took Dega labor to plant rubber and coffee. When the harvest came, they sent it to the lowlands. They used all sorts of tricks to destroy the ethnic minorities and take our land. Many Dega went to prison.

'Beginning in 1980 they started turning all the land over to the Vietnamese. Each day more and more Vietnamese arrived, by the truckload… We [FULRO] conducted a struggle in the forest to oppose them for many years. The life of Vietnamese and Montagnards together is like dogs biting each other; never easy.'

The Montagnards remain under threat from government policies in Vietnam. In 2007, for example, the prime minister's office announced the intention of eliminating all slash-and-burn agriculture by minorities. In addition, around 100,000 people from 13 different indigenous groups are under threat of resettlement to make way for the Son La dam project – the largest in Vietnam, which is set to be completed by 2015. The first groups resettled were moved to higher ground with no access to river water, where it was hard to sustain their traditional lifestyle.

There are currently over 350 Montagnard prisoners of conscience in Vietnamese jails.[4]

Refugee crises

People are often made refugees as a result of conflict. Such crises can also be triggered by 'natural' disasters such as floods and drought, and other human-made catastrophes such as ethnic cleansing and genocide. Again, indigenous peoples are highly vulnerable to becoming refugees and internally displaced persons – those forced to move within their own countries rather than across borders. Indigenous and tribal refugee populations include the estimated 150,000 Saharawi people from Western Sahara who have to live in refugee camps in Algeria because Morocco illegally occupied their lands. There are also Kurds, their land divided between four different countries (though since the 2003 invasion of Iraq they have carved out a *de facto* homeland of their own in the north of that country); Afghan tribal peoples, seeking refuge everywhere from Australia to Britain; Roma (Gypsies), fleeing persecution across Europe; the Muslim Rohingya people of Burma (Myanmar) who have fled to Bangladesh, while the Karen, Mon and other groups have gone to Thailand. The Nagas live in a state they call Nagalim, or Nagaland, on the junction between China, India and Burma; some of them have become refugees. Chakma people of the contested Chittagong Hill Tracts, Bangladesh, have sought refuge in India and Burma in their thousands. At least 50,000 Chakma were also displaced by the Kaptai Dam reservoir.

Tourism

Tourists have taken over where the early explorers left off – seeking leisure, pleasure and excitement in remote parts of the world. Now there are millions of them, and unwittingly or otherwise, they may trespass on indigenous people's territory and do other kinds of damage along the way. Unless run by and for indigenous communities on their own terms, so-called 'eco-tourism' is not any better, because it brings tourists into closer contact with indigenous peoples through 'tribal encounters'.

According to the campaigning group Tourism Concern, eviction from their homelands is one of the most serious impacts of tourism on indigenous peoples but there are other impacts too. Images of indigenous people may be used, for example to market a holiday destination without their being consulted as to whether they want tourists to come – and they may bear the brunt of the tourists' footprint when their numbers exceed sustainable levels. All too often they pay the social and environmental costs without benefiting from any of the revenue the tourists bring with them.

When the World Summit on Eco-tourism was held in Canada in 2002, only a small number of indigenous people managed to attend but they struggled successfully to introduce their concerns and perspectives into the official declaration that was taken to the World Summit on Sustainable Development later the same year.

Since then there has been increasing interest from indigenous groups around the world in trying to develop forms of alternative tourism over which they retain control. Perhaps the most successful example is in western Canada, where millions of dollars are spent each year by tourists seeking an insight into First Nations life by spending the night in a *tipi* or the day in a sweatlodge – but with indigenous people controlling the industry. According to the Aboriginal Tourism Association of British Columbia, this kind of business is booming. The non-profit organization has over 60 aboriginal companies under its auspices that cater for some 3.8 million tourists and benefit from revenues of $35 million. It has also taken on a proselytizing role, aiming to spread the word about the potential of such indigenous tourism to communities all over the world – in 2011, for example, they hosted a group from the aboriginal minority in Taiwan who were anxious to replicate the model in their own country.[5]

Negative portrayal

Derisory and negative descriptions of indigenous peoples crop up everywhere. Even in 'quality' journalism, the indigenous person can end up being the butt of a writer's joke, despite the fact that racism against, say, black or Irish people would no longer be tolerated. Countless films have used indigenous people as extras, brought in to add 'exoticism' and a dash of 'savagery', accompanied by war whoops and drumming. The following story tells how a famous movie-maker got it wrong.

X

Example: a film-maker in Peru

In 1979 the German filmmaker Werner Herzog arrived in Peru to make a film about Fitzcarraldo, the rubber baron. He had reckoned without opposition from local Aguaruna Indians. The Aguaruna Council told Herzog he could not film in indigenous territory. They did not want to take part in a piece of myth-making, in which a notoriously bloodthirsty person was portrayed as a considerate and eccentric music-lover obsessed with the idea of bringing opera to the Amazon. Herzog and his crew were sent packing from the area. This sparked a national debate in Congress that polarized opinion. The Aguaruna won the day, persuading people that men who had built their fortunes on slavery, murder and oppression of indigenous peoples should not be allowed to represent Peru. Herzog was forced to shoot the film a thousand miles south in Asháninka territory. Apparently, the Asháninka did not have the know-how or political awareness to oppose him, and the film *Fitzcarraldo* was completed with their assistance.[6]

Slavery

Modern slavery includes human trafficking, bonded and forced labor, domestic, sexual and other forms of slavery that should have been stamped out more than a century ago. Poverty, inequality and discrimination are at the root of this. Since indigenous peoples are often the poorest and least powerful of groups, they are vulnerable to being enslaved.

Example: forced labor and other abuses in Burma

Burma's military government has viciously cracked down on the pro-democracy movement in recent decades. Anyone who opposes the state is liable to face counterinsurgency operations, forced labor and relocation, the destruction of homes and crops, extra-judicial executions and other gross human rights abuses. The best-known opposition figure is movement leader

Facing the problems

Aung San Suu Kyi. But also among the victims (and the resisters) are the Karen people and other indigenous groups. About a third of the country's population consists of ethnically distinct hill peoples. There are 11 main indigenous groups, of whom the largest are the Karen, Kachin, Shan, Chin, Palaung and Naga. The Karen struggle for independence is one of the longest-running indigenous rebellions in Asia.

Tens of thousands of indigenous people have been moved out of their villages at gunpoint to relocation sites where they are forced to labor for up to 15 days a month. They are forced to build public works and infrastructure such as roads, maintain army camps and porter for army patrols. At these sites, curfews and other bans control people's free movement and free speech. Soldiers openly loot their belongings. Indigenous people have also been displaced from their villages to the forests, or to areas contested by the army and rebel groups. Army 'scorched earth' operations have aimed to flush out people hiding in the jungle. Soldiers shoot on sight. Thousands of indigenous people have fled the country to become refugees.

Language

There are around 6,500 languages in the world today, of which more than half – many of them spoken by indigenous peoples – face the threat of extinction this century. This has been called the linguistic equivalent of an ecological disaster.

According to recent research, the five regions where languages are disappearing most rapidly are: northern Australia, central South America, North America's upper Pacific coastal zone, eastern Siberia, and Oklahoma and the southwestern United States. All of these regions are inhabited by indigenous people with falling numbers speaking their own language.[7]

One example of an endangered language is Tofa, spoken only by about 60 reindeer herders and hunters in central Siberia. Tofa has hardly ever been written down, but it has a rich oral tradition of epic poems, stories, proverbs and songs. In Turkey, the ban on education and broadcasts in Kurdish was finally lifted in 2002 after years of repression, as Turkey groomed itself for EU membership.

Languages are under threat because success, in many societies, can only be achieved through speaking and writing the dominant language, such as English, Russian or Turkish. In many countries, indigenous or minority languages are banned in schools which follow a curriculum in the dominant, national language. Languages can only survive if they are passed from parents to children, and many parents are now choosing not to do so. 'Every language is the repository of the culture of the people who speak it,' says Nigel Vincent, Professor of Linguistics at the University of Manchester. 'When we lose a language, we lose something of the world's diversity.'[8]

Health and disease

Indigenous peoples are vulnerable to diseases linked to poverty, including diabetes, heart and lung disease, malnutrition and HIV/AIDS. If little or no basic primary healthcare exists within reach, people die from easily preventable illness. Another factor is people's distrust of state health services, especially if they are staffed by whites or people who speak a different language. The sick may prefer to be treated with 'traditional' medicine in a more informal place. As a result of outside contact, people's diets have often changed for the worse, with sugary, processed, over-salted, additive- and pesticide-laced foods replacing the traditional ones. So they are now more vulnerable to illnesses linked to Western diet.

There are high rates of alcoholism in some indigenous communities – a barometer of social breakdown, unemployment and despair. Drunkenness by non-whites is often used as an excuse for arrest and conviction, for example among Australian Aboriginals, who suffer

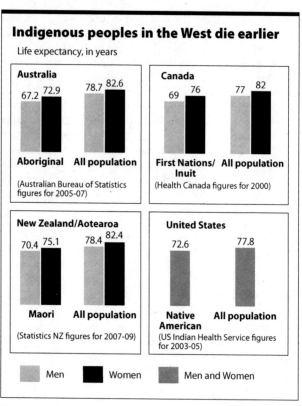

Indigenous peoples in the West die earlier

Life expectancy, in years

Australia

67.2   72.9   78.7   82.6

Aboriginal   **All population**

(Australian Bureau of Statistics figures for 2005-07)

Canada

69   76   77   82

First Nations/ Inuit   **All population**

(Health Canada figures for 2000)

New Zealand/Aotearoa

70.4   75.1   78.4   82.4

Maori   **All population**

(Statistics NZ figures for 2007-09)

United States

72.6   77.8

Native American   **All population**

(US Indian Health Service figures for 2003-05)

Men   Women   Men and Women

disproportionately high rates of arrest for minor offenses. Substance abuse is also on the rise, particularly petrol sniffing. A 1990 government inquiry showed that Aboriginal people are disproportionately likely to die from pneumonia, gastroenteritis, other diarrheal diseases, cirrhosis of the liver, pancreatitis, cot death and road accidents. Two white-introduced diseases – trachoma and leprosy – are still rife in Aboriginal communities years after they have disappeared in white ones.

There is a similar story in the Americas. Among Native Americans, the incidence of almost every known communicable disease is far higher compared with the population as a whole, infectious diseases are more likely to prove fatal, and alcoholism is the bane of many reservations. Tuberculosis rates in Canada show a stark distinction between the health of the indigenous and non-indigenous populations.

AIDS is the 'new' scourge, largely affecting poor people in the South. It is impossible to give a breakdown of the numbers of indigenous peoples affected, because testing is not globally available and many people do not come forward anyway. But it is a particular danger in communities where women and girls are powerless to negotiate safe sex; in conflicts and refugee crises; where

Aboriginal health in crisis

While health conditions for indigenous peoples in Canada, New Zealand/Aotearoa and the US have improved since the 1980s, in Australia they have actually deteriorated. The *Sydney Morning Herald* on 16 November 2009 said that 'Australia is the only place on the planet where indigenous health and wellbeing are going backwards' and talked of 'a shamed nation' turning 'a blind eye'.

● Death rates for Australian indigenous people are around three times higher than for the non-indigenous.

● Babies born to indigenous women are much more likely to die in their first year than those born to non-indigenous women. Whereas the total Australian infant mortality rate was 4.1 deaths per 1,000 births in 2008, the infant mortality rate for indigenous babies ranged between almost 14 in Northern Territory and almost 7 in South Australia.

● Diabetes is around three-and-a-half times more common among indigenous people than among other Australians.

● End-stage renal disease was almost nine times more common for indigenous people than for non-indigenous people in 2004-07.

● Indigenous males were 5.8 times more likely and indigenous females 3.1 times more likely to die from mental and behavioral disorders between 2001 and 2005 than their non-indigenous counterparts.

● The rate of newly diagnosed cases of tuberculosis for indigenous people in 2003-07 was more than 10 times the rate for non-indigenous people.

Source: healthinfonet.ecu.edu.au/health-facts/summary

sex trafficking is rife; where traditional sexual practices are conducive to high rates of sexually transmitted disease; where there is increased urbanization and migrant labor movement; where mass tourism involves buying and selling sex alongside safaris; and where women desperate to feed their families may exchange sex for food.

The stolen children

To its infinite shame, the Australian government once had a policy of forcibly taking Aboriginal children (particularly those of mixed-race) from their families and placing them in boarding schools or with white adoptive parents. It formed part of Australia's 'assimilation policy' in the 1950s and 1960s. These children became known as the 'Stolen Generations'. Lowitja O'Donoghue, first chair of the Aboriginal and Torres Strait Islander Commission and the first indigenous regional director for the country's Department of Aboriginal Affairs, described in a 1997 speech what it was like to be 'stolen':

'The moral issues are that it's not just family life that is disrupted by these policies – it's the whole sense of individual and community identity and the repercussions that are felt by later generations. I have personal experience of this.

In 1932... I was born at Granite Downs Station in the Pitjantjatjara lands in the north-west of South Australia. My father was an Irish station manager and my mother was a Yankunjatjara woman. When I was two years of age, I was taken from my mother and placed in the Colebrooke Home – a church mission in the town of Quorn in the Flinders Ranges – where my four sisters and one brother already lived.

None of us ever saw our father again. We were forbidden to speak our traditional language or to talk about our origins, and I learned a new culture and the new name that came with it – "Lois". As I grew older, I learned about our family from my brothers and sisters, and I resolved I would one day find our mother. It took me 30 years to achieve that goal, but it was supremely important for me to fulfill it. The problem was that when I did meet my mother again, we no longer had a common language and I was unable to speak with her.'

On 13 February 2008, the then Prime Minister of Australia, Kevin Rudd, issued a formal apology to the Stolen Generations, which was subsequently passed by both houses of the Australian parliament.

Being over-researched

The text below was specially written by Moronga Tanago, a member of the Bugakhwe San people of southern Africa, who is a board member of the Working Group of Indigenous Minorities in Southern Africa (WIMSA) working with TOCADI (Trust for Okavango Culture and Development Initiatives) on culture and education. He begins by talking about the wider problems faced by San people.

'It has been a great pleasure for me to have this opportunity to air my feelings as a San person about the problems that our people are facing. Though San people live right across southern Africa, we all face similar problems. One of the biggest is the loss of our ancestral lands. Everywhere the San people have been pushed off or removed from their land by others… And the San have no power to fight this.

Because of their land loss the San people are the poorest in their countries, they struggle with education and with the problems other people brought, such as sickness and alcohol and drugs. But lately the other issue the San people are dealing with is that researchers have been studying them just for the sake of getting their PhDs. The San people feel that these researchers have been benefiting from the information they got from the San people, but the San do not feel as if they have benefited in any way from the information they have been giving out for such a long time. For example, some researchers worked on our languages or studied our ways of life, things which are very vital for us to use in future, and for the younger generation to know about. Unfortunately, we are often unable to access the information these researchers have taken from us because they write them in their own languages. Or when they write in ours they say it is too expensive to reproduce copies or books for our communities.

The very important point that I would like to share is that people must understand that we, the San, are now organized. We have our own organizations and networks that link us across the countries we live in. WIMSA networks with other San organizations in the region. The organization I work for is part of this network and others.

Honestly, the San are only asking any person who does research or who wants to write about us, film us or use our cultural goods in any way, to respect these networks and contact us through WIMSA, because we now have policies and a contract for media and research purposes. In fact, people who fail to do so will in future not receive any help or agreement from San communities. Our main aim is that the San should also benefit from the information they give out and the hospitality they have offered to other people over so many years. We are not only talking about books, copies of films, tapes etc., but also information that we can use to strengthen ourselves to hold out against the pressures of the modern times and the politics in our countries. We want to see that information work for us. This is the last chance for the San to preserve something of our own identity and knowledge, since we have lost so much of it already through our contact with other people. I hope that anyone who reads this piece will enjoy knowing more about us, but also face the challenges that we lay before you.'

Indigenous peoples are not simply victims, as Moronga makes abundantly clear. The next chapter describes some of the vibrant resistance movements, past and present, and people's individual and collective achievements on the road to rights for all.

---

1 From an 'Open Letter to the Canadian People' by Barabaig leaders, quoted in Charles Lane, *Pastures Lost*, Initiatives Publishers, 1996. **2** Partly adapted from accounts by Survival International, which has campaigned for and with the Yanomami since the 1970s, and other web sources such as: crystalinks.com/ yanomami **3** Based, with the author's permission, on a paper by Dr Ben Knighton, and updated from Minority Rights Group's website. **4** Testimony from 'A history of resistance to central government control', in a series of reports on repression of Montagnards, Human Rights Watch, viewable at hrw.org/reports/2002/vietnam Last section from Minority Rights Group. **5** *The Independent*, 17 Sep 2011, nin.tl/nUMtDu. **6** From a case study in John Beauclerk and Jeremy Narby with Janet Townsend, *Indigenous Peoples: a fieldguide for development*, Oxfam 1988. **7** nytimes.com/2007/09/19/science/19language.html **8** From David Ward, 'Language cull could leave people speechless', *The Guardian*, 25 May 2002.

5 Fighting back

Here the focus is on protest and resistance by indigenous people over the centuries – including folk heroes from the struggle all over the world. Resistance is reaching a peak in the early 21st century, with flashpoints from Kenya to Peru, Australia to the Philippines. This is the story of *Avatar* – but for real.

ON 25 JUNE 1876, above the Little Bighorn River in what is today Montana, a force of Lakota and Cheyenne warriors destroyed General George Custer and 255 soldiers of the US Seventh Cavalry in what has been called 'the last great Indian triumph in American history'.[1] The battle of Little Bighorn – Custer's Last Stand – is possibly the most famous clash ever between whites and Native Americans, if not between Europeans and indigenous peoples anywhere. Psychologically, it was a coup, the indigenous equivalent of David beating Goliath. Inevitably, however, it led to a vicious payback: white leaders and soldiers vowed to wipe out the 'Indian'. There was a similar story across colonial Africa, where many indigenous and tribal peoples tried to resist Europeans with spears and arrows, only to be brutally put down in most cases. Military tit for tat rarely leads to real victory in the end. Violent protest has had its uses but it should not overshadow the many other forms of indigenous resistance that have been used with mixed success before and since.

The Aborigines' Protection Society (APS) was launched in London in 1837 by prominent abolitionists of slavery who realized that emancipation had not cured the problem of European exploitation of indigenous peoples. The first African branch (called the Aborigines' Rights Protection Society, ARPS) was set up in the Gold Coast (now Ghana), West Africa, in 1897. Similar African groups followed. In the early days, 'Aborigine' simply referred to non-whites, and not necessarily First Peoples. The two great features of these organizations in

Africa were that they provided an alternative route to London for complainants, who could get inconvenient questions asked about the treatment of colonized Africans by sympathetic members of parliament. The official route was no good because it went through the colonial hierarchy. Second, their very existence gave hope to colonized peoples and those who sided with them. Even in countries where there were no branches, such as South Africa, a network of correspondents kept London informed. Some of these whistle-blowers were themselves colonial officials. The APS largely concentrated on the colonies, while the closely linked British and Foreign Anti-Slavery Society (founded 1839) dealt with territories outside the empire. In 1909, they merged to become the Anti-Slavery and Aborigines' Protection Society, the crusading organization today called Anti-Slavery International.[2]

Much earlier, in the US, indigenous leaders used formal legal channels to assert their rights to land. The Mohegan land case, for example, went to the Privy Council in London in 1765. The Mohegan were struggling to reclaim lands illegally seized by the colony of Connecticut. Their spokesperson, Samson Occom, toured Britain for two years from 1765, preaching 300 sermons and raising more than £12,000 for the cause. Unhappily for them, the Privy Council dismissed the case. In 1833, a Pequot 'Indian' preacher and writer, William Apess, led the Mashpee Revolt in protest against the unfair laws of Massachusetts. The Mashpee won most of their demands, and Apess became a national figure. Other later legal cases included the unsuccessful eight-year court battle by the Montauk Indians from Long Island, launched in 1909. They wanted to regain their land title and keep developers out. The developers argued that the Montauk were no longer an 'Indian tribe' because they had intermarried with African-Americans and taken up a modern lifestyle. The judge agreed, and threw the case out.

Fighting back

Back in Africa, colonial Kenya was the scene of an extraordinary case brought by the Maasai in 1913. With the help of British lawyers, they took the British government to court to challenge the legality of land snatching and win reparations for land and stock losses suffered during a forced move (see *Folk hero: Parsaloi Ole Gilisho*). Again, they lost on a flimsy pretext – but their battle continues today. Modern campaigners have been encouraged by a victory scored by Maasai and Samburu from northern Kenya in July 2002. The British Ministry of Defence agreed to pay £4.5 million (then $6.7 million) compensation plus legal costs to 228 pastoralists who were bereaved or injured by British army explosives left lying around on their grazing land after military exercises.

In the colonial period, indigenous and tribal peoples took to litigation after petitions and other peaceful means failed. Early petitions and delegations to London included those by Maori to Queen Victoria before the 1840 Waitangi Treaty, when they complained about the damage being done to Maori land and culture by settlers and land speculators. Aborigines on Flinders

---

Folk hero: Parsaloi Ole Gilisho, Kenya

Ole Gilisho was an unsung African Geronimo. In 1911-13, when he was an illiterate warrior, he led a peaceful rebellion against the British colonial government that was trying to force the pastoralist Maasai people out of their ancestral lands into reserves to make way for white settlers. The British expected violent resistance. Instead, Ole Gilisho surprised them by hiring British lawyers and, with the help of a British doctor called Norman Leys, took the government to court to challenge the forced moves and land losses. The so-called Maasai Case of 1913 was lost on a technicality. But it was a landmark legal action for its time and place – probably the first time indigenous peoples in this part of Africa had challenged the legality of colonial oppression and land snatching. The Maasai lost the case and up to 70 per cent of their land. But Ole Gilisho is remembered today as a selfless hero who put the welfare of his beloved people first, and used modern legal processes to take on the colonizers. ∎

Some landmark dates for the indigenous movement

(IP = indigenous peoples)

1920s Alaskan Native Brotherhood and Society for American Indians formed

1923 Indigenous leader Deskaheh, from the Iroquois Confederacy, unsuccessfully seeks help from the League of Nations, Geneva, in their dispute with the Canadian government

1957 ILO Convention 107, first international instrument covering IP – but no IP were consulted in the drafting

1968 International Work Group for Indigenous Affairs (IWGIA) set up

1974-5 American Indian Treaty Council established in the US (now called International Indian Treaty Council)

1977 World Council of Indigenous Peoples set up, Canada; First international NGO conference on IP issues, Geneva

1982 UN establishes Working Group on Indigenous Populations

1984 Coordinating Body for Indigenous Organizations of the Amazon Basin (COICA) formed

1986 India launches its first Tribal and Indigenous Council

1989 ILO Convention 169 replaces the 1957 Convention

1992 UN Conference on Environment and Development (UNCED): the Rio Declaration recognizes indigenous peoples' role in environmental protection

1992 Asia Indigenous Peoples Pact formed to represent Asian IP

1992 Rigoberta Menchú (Maya Indian from Guatemala) wins Nobel Peace Prize

1993 World Conference on Human Rights: the Vienna Declaration and Programme of Action recommend that the UN General Assembly proclaim a UN Decade for Indigenous Peoples, establish the Permanent Forum on Indigenous Issues and adopt a declaration on indigenous rights

1995-2004 UN International Decade of the World's Indigenous Peoples

1998 The UN Commission on Human Rights sets up the Ad-Hoc Working Group on the establishment of the Permanent Forum

2000 Permanent Forum on Indigenous Issues established

May 2002 First meeting of the Permanent Forum, New York

2005-2014 Second UN Decade of the World's Indigenous Peoples

2006 Indigenous leader Evo Morales becomes president of Bolivia

2007 The Declaration on the Rights of Indigenous Peoples is passed by the UN General Assembly, with only four countries voting against. The UN Working Group on Indigenous Populations is restructured as the Expert Mechanism on the Rights of Indigenous Peoples.

Island in the Bass Strait petitioned the Queen in 1846. Lobengula, king of the Ndebele in what is now Zimbabwe, sent two representatives to London in 1889 to beg for protection against land grabbers and gold diggers led by Cecil Rhodes. They returned with royal greetings, but no protection. The Griqua of South Africa also appealed for British protection in the 1860s, in the face of a land takeover by diamond miners. This failed, and they rebelled in 1878. Swazi envoys went to London in 1894 to ask Queen Victoria to protect Swaziland against the Boers; their petition was also refused. A series of petitions and delegations by South African chiefs to King George V in the 1900s asked him to veto aggressive new laws that took land and rights away from black people.

The indigenous movement really took off in the 1960s and 1970s. Its rapid growth coincided with the independence struggles of colonized peoples, decolonization, the rise of Red Power in North America and Black Power in the US and Australia in particular, the flowering of the human rights movement and of the UN. The movement became increasingly international, with the setting up of the International Indian Treaty Council in 1974 in the US and the World Council of Indigenous Peoples in 1977 in Canada. These two bodies helped to initiate the first international conference of non-governmental organizations (NGOs) on indigenous issues in 1977 in Geneva, which effectively launched the global indigenous movement. The last two decades of the 20th century saw a groundswell of politicized indigenous activity across Africa, South America, Asia, the Pacific and elsewhere, linked to the explosion of civil society organizations (CSOs) among the world's poor, and the declining power of some states.[3]

Today, many of the protests link to anti-globalization campaigning. The collective enemy now is the kind of modern imperialism that forces its agenda, values,

Folk hero: Rigoberta Menchú Tum, Guatemala

Rigoberta Menchú is a Mayan-Quiche activist who was awarded the Nobel Peace Prize in 1992, the youngest person and the first indigenous person ever to receive it. Besides promoting peace she has fought all her life for indigenous and women's rights, global education and universal justice. Despite little schooling, Rigoberta was politically active from an early age – as soon as she was old enough to accompany her father to meetings of a local peasant activists' group. Her resolve deepened after her parents and two brothers were tortured and killed by the military in the early 1980s, during a time of government crackdown on 'communist guerrillas'. Rigoberta had to flee to Mexico, where she spoke out against repression in Guatemala. She gave talks across the Americas, calling for peace in her country and justice for indigenous peoples. She has raised global awareness of the issues, and set up a foundation to promote peace, indigenous rights and other causes. In 2006 she co-founded the Nobel Women's Peace Initiative to work for peace with justice and equality as well as women's rights. She stood in the 2011 presidential elections in Guatemala as the candidate of the Frente Amplio, a leftist alliance, but was defeated by former general Otto Peréz Molina. ∎

armies, bombs and products on other societies. Indigenous protest also feeds into other types of wider activism, such as the Landless Workers' Movement (MST) in Brazil and the 'nuclear free' movement in the Pacific. But globalization in its broadest sense also has its uses, since indigenous protesters are increasingly using the internet to make contacts, link up, and put pressure on governments and the corporate sector. A wealth of information about indigenous peoples' protest movements is available on the web. It is fast, furious and successful – making up for past losses, when a lack of literacy and access to technology meant that many protests went unheard.

One of the issues that has been much discussed online over recent years has been the call for the repatriation of human remains and other artifacts stolen from indigenous peoples.

Fighting back

Bones of contention

Museums are coming under increasing pressure to give up their collections of indigenous human remains. Many acquired these collections in the Victorian and Edwardian eras, when travelers, scientists and trophy-hunters collected bodies and body parts from far-flung places to put on display in the West. Indigenous groups want the body parts returned home for a decent burial.

There have long been calls for the return of such treasures as Greece's Elgin marbles and Benin's bronzes, but the dead are a different class altogether because their display is obviously offensive and upsetting to the living. Museums are also uneasy about the dubious way in which they acquired these collections. For example, the Natural History Museum in London, which has 20,000 body parts, possesses a skull and leg bone from a young man who was shot in 1900 near Victoria River, Australia, during a so-called punitive raid. The collector 'prepared' the bones on the spot, boiling off the skin in a cooking pot.

Museums in the UK began to receive requests for the repatriation of indigenous remains in the mid-1980s, mainly from Australian Aboriginal groups. Among the organizations campaigning for their return were the Tasmanian Aboriginal Centre and the Foundation for Aboriginal and Islander Research Action. The pressure continued through the 1990s and led in 1997, for example, to the return of Tasmanian hair samples from Edinburgh University, a Tasmanian skull from Stockholm and the skull of Yagan, a Western Australian warrior shot and beheaded in 1833, from a Liverpool cemetery. In 2000, Edinburgh University repatriated its remaining collection of Aboriginal remains, and its collection of Hawaiian remains.

The constant pressure from indigenous groups on the issue led the British Labour government to review its policy and resulted in 2006 in a new law, the Human

Tissue Act, which allows museums to return remains that are believed to be under 1,000 years in age. The Culture Minister at the time, David Lammy, said the British government had changed the law in 'response to the claims of indigenous peoples, particularly in Australia, for the return of ancestral remains'. Curators of the country's main museums, including the British Museum and the Natural History Museum, also supported the legal change. A spokesperson for the British Museum said the institution was committed to returning human remains provided that Aboriginal communities could prove their connection.

Since the British law change, the numbers of remains returned has increased and there seems to be something of a global trend – the Smithsonian Institution in Washington became the first US museum to respond when it returned the remains of 33 indigenous Australians to Arnhem Land in 2008.

In 2011, Britain's Natural History Museum returned to Australia the remains of 138 indigenous Torres Strait Islanders. Ned David, a community leader from the islands, said that he was 'deeply touched' by the museum's decision, which followed a long campaign by Aboriginal leaders. As part of the arrangement, the Museum offered a placement to a Torres Strait Islander so as to enable it to understand better the culture of indigenous peoples.

Indigenous campaigners welcomed the new British legislation as a sign that the repatriation of remains had moved into the political sphere in Europe as it already had in Australia more than a decade before. Activists still demand increased access to collection documentation – something many museums are wary of. Without being able to see the archives, indigenous communities cannot find out whose remains are being held. The question of what to do with remains whose origin is unclear is one of the biggest problems around repatriation.

Fighting back

Within Australia, there have been major restitutions since the government adopted national policies on repatriating remains. The main one is the Strategic Plan for the Return of Indigenous Ancestral Remains, unveiled in 1998, which does not apply to collections overseas.

In the US, repatriation is largely covered by the Native American Graves Protection and Repatriation Act (NAGPRA), 1990. It protects burial sites on federal and tribal lands and creates a process for repatriating cultural items, including artifacts and human remains, to 'tribes'. In 1993, museums holding Native American artifacts were ordered to make written summaries of their collections for distribution to people culturally linked to the artifacts; in 1995, they were told to make detailed inventories. These and other developments have increased tensions between Native American activists, academics and archeologists. The ongoing rows include arguments over Kennewick Man, a 9,200-year-old body found in Kennewick, Washington, in 1996. Should scientists be allowed to study his remains, or should he be allowed to rest in peace on Native American land? In 2004, the US Court of Appeals for the Ninth Circuit ruled that the link between Kennewick Man and indigenous groups could not be genetically proven and so allowed scientists to continue to study the remains, which are technically the property of the US Army Corps of Engineers, on whose land they were found.

The Richtersveld land claim

When the ANC government took power following South Africa's first free elections in 1994, it enacted a new constitution that promised land reform and land restitution. The Nama indigenous inhabitants of what had been formerly known as a 'Coloured Rural Reserve' in the Richtersveld, an arid region of the Northern Cape, took them at their word and claimed their ancestral land. The court case ran from 1998 and had many phases. It was first rejected by the Land Claims Court but the Supreme Court and the Constitutional Court accepted the people's claim that they had owned land under indigenous law prior to the annexation of Namaqualand in 1847 – that they retained rights that had previously been rejected on the grounds of their 'race and lack of civilization'. The successful claim includes rights to minerals and precious stones on the land – and thus to restitution for those extracted since 1927 by the mining company Alexkor, which was owned by the South African government. It also allows for the rehabilitation of land damaged by mining – or for compensation for damage where rehabilitation is impossible.

In a 2002 referendum, the residents were asked if the deed of ownership to the land should be handed over to the community itself, to local government or carved up in pieces for individual ownership. The vote was overwhelmingly for the community option and a Communal Property Association was set up.

The legal victory was celebrated all over the world as a landmark case for indigenous rights. Sadly, the story since has not been entirely positive. In 2007, 2,000 beneficiaries each received a one-off payment of 1,500 Rand ($180). But the bulk of the compensation money remains locked due to a legal dispute between the leadership of the Communal Property Association and a group of dissidents backed by Cape Town company Uhuru Communications. The dissidents claim the Communal Property Association's leadership are guilty of nepotism and are insufficiently accountable, while others suspect the constant legal challenges stem from Uhuru's wish to muscle in on potential future profits.

The mining company Alexkor has also been through a moribund period. But its mining rights on land were finally transferred to the local community in April 2011 and a joint venture in which the community has a

49-per-cent stake duly established. In the wake of this, the company announced its first profit for five years in September 2011.

Land struggles: the Ogiek in Kenya

In Kenya, Ogiek people are fighting attempts by their own government to evict them from the Mau forests to the west of the Rift Valley. The Mau is vital to Kenyan ecology as the largest closed-canopy forest ecosystem in the country and one of its five main 'water towers'. Hunter-gatherers who claim to have lived in these forests for centuries, they have taken the government to court over the future of the Mau forests. The 20,000-strong Ogiek argue that they have lived in the forest ecosystem as hunter-gatherers for centuries, over which time they have been a force for conservation rather than for deforestation or degradation. If evicted, the Ogiek face destitution. Over the years, many Ogiek have been forcibly evicted from the forest and now live in poverty on its borders. It is estimated that 10,000 Ogiek still live within the forest, dependent upon it for their livelihood.

In 2010, the Ogiek renewed their efforts to secure their rights and their future, forming a 60-strong Ogiek Council of Elders that could negotiate with the government. There has been no major progress, however, despite the new Kenyan constitution of August 2010, which was a huge step forward in recognizing indigenous rights. The constitution recognizes the marginalization of indigenous groups in language that is close to that of the UN Declaration on the Rights of Indigenous Peoples. It defines a marginalized community as one that 'out of need or desire to preserve its unique culture and identity from assimilation, has remained outside the integrated social and economic life of Kenya as a whole, or an indigenous community that has retained and maintained a traditional lifestyle and livelihood based on a hunter or gatherer economy'.

The constitution requires the state to enable adequate representation of such 'marginalized groups at all levels of government and to pursue affirmative action on their behalf. The Ogiek are still waiting for the evidence that these commitments are more than just words.[4]

Struggling against dams: Peru's Asháninka

The Asháninka people of the Ene-Tambo river basin have good reason to be distrustful. Over the years they have had their quota of outsiders after gold or wood or oil or human souls to save. In the mid-1980s, Maoist guerrillas of Sendero Luminoso (Shining Path) turned up, gained control and a long nightmare began.

Peru's two decades of violence took an especially heavy toll on the Asháninka. Out of a total population of 70,000, around 6,000 were killed or 'disappeared'. Thousands more were displaced, up to 40 communities destroyed or abandoned. Both the guerrillas and the army used and abused Asháninka people, and communities were set against each other. Sendero pressed children as well as adults into their ranks and carried out gruesome punishments against those who resisted. Many died of hunger. The army, for its part, would send Asháninka ahead of them when trying to root out the guerrillas hiding in the forests.[2] As the violence intensified, entire communities had to be airlifted to safety. They were only able to start returning to their land in the late 1990s.

As of the 2010s, once more, the Asháninka people are on the frontline. Their main adversary is the institution that should be protecting them – the State.

Under a 50-year energy agreement signed in 2010, Peru will allow Brazil to build six dams in the Amazon to generate electricity for Brazil. The 2,000-megawatt Pakitzapango plant would be one of the first to generate power for utility giant Electrobraz. Two more, Tambo 40 and Tambo 60, are planned for the adjoining River Tambo.

Legally, Asháninka land is protected. But at no point did the Peruvian authorities or the companies involved consult the people affected by the Pakitzapango scheme. This is in plain contravention of both the UN Declaration on the Rights of Indigenous Peoples and ILO Convention 169, which insists that no major development should go ahead without 'free, prior and informed consent' of affected residents.

Shutting down the Santa Ana mine: Peru

'The Santa Ana project is located 140 kilometers south of the city of Puno in the department of Puno,' said the website of the Vancouver-based Bear Creek Mining Corporation in early 2011, describing the new silver mine it was about to open up.

'Relations with the local communities in the region are favorable,' it continued, 'and the company is working closely with the local communities to ensure the project is developed to maximize long term sustainable growth in the region.'

Not surprisingly, that part of the website has been taken down now because, from late March, the region was convulsed for 45 days as thousands of people rose up to protest against this project.

Highland communities near the small town of Huacallani complained they had not been properly consulted and that the mine would ruin their environment and their livelihoods dependent on growing quinoa and potatoes and rearing alpacas. Their message was clear: 'Agro si, mina no!' ('Agriculture yes, mining no!')

The protest spread like wildfire. An estimated 25,000 people were mobilized. The regional capital, Puno, came to a standstill as an indefinite strike was declared. Main highways were blocked with boulders, including the busy frontier with Bolivia at Desaguadero.

After seven weeks of unrest, costing an estimated $117 million, the outgoing government of Alan Garcia took the uncharacteristic step of revoking Bear Creek's license, on the grounds that the Santa Ana mine was 'no longer in the national interest'.

As the protest spread several local mayors gave their backing, as did students, churches and even professional bodies such as Puno's architects.

Women played a key role, often on the front line, but also serving up food in large pots.

'We are all against the mine,' said Aymara grandmother Concepcion

The main Asháninka organization, CARE (Central Asháninka River Ene), took legal action and the company that was supposed to be doing the initial feasibility studies did not get its license renewed. But the option remains for another company to step in. And the prospect of a second big dam came one step closer in November 2010, when the Brazilian construction giant Odebrecht was granted a license for Tambo 40.

In the words of CARE's president Ruth Buendia: 'With Paquitzapango and Tambo 40 comes terrorism,

---

Consechoke. 'We left our children and our fields and brought our soups and our potatoes. It was very cold at night and some people had to be taken to hospital. In the main square [of Puno] some people insulted and threatened us. But we are the people who look after the land, who defend nature. The governments, the authorities have sold us. I am old but I will strike again if necessary. I want us to go forward and fight. I don't want them to poison us, to poison our children.'

Miriam Ramirez, a peasant organizer from the indigenous Quechua community said: 'The Aymaras started it but we Quechuas were ready to support. We were warned that we would get shot if we went on strike again but we are prepared to die.'

Few indigenous or community leaders are calling for an absolute ban on all mining. But they want a national plan that at least outlines which areas are considered suitable for such activities and which are not.

The communities also want international standards to be applied: activist Pepe Julio Gutierrez points out that while Canada and Australia prohibit cyanide, their mining companies operating in Peru use it. There are similar double standards on the use of dynamite and open-cast methods that cause air pollution.

But the protesting communities have shown that they too have power: to effectively mobilize. Halting Santa Ana was not the only victory. Protesters also managed to get Brazilian Egasur's dam project at Inambari in the lowlands of Puno shelved. A couple of months earlier, the strength of protest led to the suspension of Southern Peru Copper Corporation's license to open a new mine at Tia Maria, Arequipa. In each case social movements came together to powerfully reject a form of development based on ecologically harmful resource extraction. What is certain is that indigenous-led protest in Peru is not over by a long chalk.

Vanessa Baird, *New Internationalist*, October 2011.

not armed now, but economic.'

There are alternatives to the extractive model, better suited to the Amazon. For example, the area is rich in biological diversity and medicinal plants. Trade in more eco-friendly natural forest products could be developed. Community tourism is another potential area for sustainable development. There are energy alternatives, too: Peru has a high potential for both wind and solar power, while small-scale community owned hydropower has a long and proven record for meeting local needs.

So far there is little indication that Peru's new left-leaning president, Ollanta Humala, is prepared to abandon the development path of his predecessors,

---

Folk hero: Alberto Pizango, Peru

Alberto Pizango made international news in 2009, in connection with the massacre at Bagua when police clashed with indigenous Awajun Wambis protesters and more than 30 people lost their lives. Pizango, who is president of AIDESEP, the umbrella movement for indigenous groups in the Amazon, was accused by the authorities of 'sedition'. Fearing for his life, he fled into exile in Nicaragua. He returned to face trial in May 2010, but charges were dropped in June 2011. There is talk of his being a candidate for the 2016 presidential election.

'The current, non-indigenous structure of representative democracy minimizes the possibilities of living together and in harmony with nature. We propose a system that is real democracy, in which it is the people who give orders and the government that obeys.

'Our movement aims to be a model at a global level. All are invited to partake. We want to make the big leap into what it means to be a citizen of the planet. Planetary citizenship is our ideal. To us the human body is like the planet and the planet is like a human body. We have been accused of being romantic, but I say we are being practical. This is reality. Reality is what we touch, it's what we smell in the fresh earth, free from contamination.

'The political project for a harmonious development that we are constructing is in opposition to the politics of the West which promotes development that persists in being inequitable, that fails to respect the rights of human beings, that is killing life and accelerating disaster. ' ∎

but he is perceived as being more open to listening to indigenous and other groups.

There are signs of hope. In June 2011, plans for a giant dam at Inambari were shelved after massive, paralyzing protests in the Puno area (see box). If the clamor against Pakitzapango, Tambo 40 and the other mega-dams being planned can reach a similar pitch, then anything is possible.

The struggle of the Asháninka is theirs but not theirs alone – it should be that of all of us. Quite apart from the moral requirement to take a stand against the ongoing abuse of indigenous human rights, we all need a healthy Amazon, the lungs of the world, for planetary survival.[5]

Struggle for self-rule: the Kanaks

The Kanaks are what indigenous Melanesian people call themselves. On the islands of Kanaky (New Caledonia) in the Pacific, they have been struggling to throw off the colonial yoke ever since the French annexed the islands in 1853. A French military regime ruled New Caledonia for the rest of the century. Colonialism was a bitter experience. Dispossessed of their lands and decimated, the Kanaks became a powerless 'minority' in their own land, even though they make up about 44 per cent of the population today. They did not get the right to vote until 1957. The struggle continues over land and political power, and has become increasingly violent.

Kanaky/New Caledonia is still a French Overseas Territory. The years 1984-86 saw political turmoil and violence, known simply as 'Les Evénements' (The Events). Independence parties, disillusioned by the French government's empty promises of reform, launched the FLNKS (Front de Libération National Kanak et Socialiste). Its first leader was Jean-Marie Tjibaou. Violence broke out when the FLNKS boycotted the 1984 election, and one of its leaders was shot by paramilitaries. France flew in troops and declared a six-month state of emergency. In 1986 the UN put Kanaky back on its decolonization list, which gave hope to the independence movement. But France accused the UN of meddling in its internal affairs and expelled the Australian consul-general from the islands, saying he had played a leading role in this. Tjibaou was assassinated in 1989 by a splinter group of Kanaks who claimed that the FLNKS had sold out.

A referendum is due to take place between 2014 and 2019 to decide whether New Caledonia remains part of France or whether Kanaky becomes an independent state. In July 2010, the Kanak flag was adopted as a dual official national flag, to be flown alongside the French tricolore.

Folk hero: Geronimo, North America

Also known as Goyathlay (pronounced Goyahkla and meaning 'one who yawns'), Geronimo is remembered as a formidable warrior and survivor who waged many battles with the US military. He was one of several outstanding leaders of the Apache people, among the first and last tribes to resist white encroachment. Born in 1829 in what is today Western New Mexico, he lost his entire family – including his mother, young wife Alope and three children – when Mexican troops attacked their camp. This mass murder, in the 1850s, led to a burning desire for vengeance and Geronimo's life-long hatred of Mexicans. Ironically, it was Mexican soldiers who gave him the name Geronimo, now synonymous with indigenous struggle. He played cat and mouse with a US government agent called John Clum, who was obsessed with the idea of arresting and hanging the 'troublemaker'. On many occasions, when the noose was tightening around him, he miraculously threw off his pursuers and escaped from under their noses. In 1875 all Apaches west of the Rio Grande were ordered into a reservation. Geronimo escaped from the reservation three times and always managed to avoid capture. A shaman, he believed he had been given special powers to resist the white man's weapons; he certainly survived many gunshot wounds and held out the longest of all Native Americans. He died in Alabama in 1909 as a prisoner of war, unable to return to his homeland. When he surrendered in 1886, Geronimo said: 'Once I moved about like the wind. Now I surrender to you and that is all… My heart is yours and I hope yours will be mine.' ■

Folk hero: Louis Riel, Canada

Louis Riel was a Métis (indigenous person of mixed ancestry) who led the only armed resistance ever against the state in the Canadian North-West. Born in 1844 in the Red River Settlement in what is now Manitoba, he began training as a priest and then as a lawyer, but never completed either. He tried to set up an independent Métis state, after heading a provisional government from 1869-70. His involvement in the execution of Thomas Scott, one of a group sent to overthrow the rebels, led to his exile from Canada. While in exile he spent some time in an asylum, and came to believe he had a religious mission to lead the Métis people. In 1885, the Métis again declared a breakaway government. Riel led a short-lived armed rebellion that year, but was forced to surrender to Canadian forces. He was put on trial for treason, rejecting attempts by his lawyer to find him not guilty by reason of insanity. The jury found him guilty but recommended mercy. Judge Richardson had other ideas, and sentenced him to death. He was hanged in November 1885, which caused outrage across Quebec. ■

Trick or treaty?

Some colonial treaties were not entirely bad news for indigenous peoples, since they recognized indigenous sovereignty. These can sometimes be used today to win reparations and prove separate nationhood. But others (such as the Waitangi Treaty made between the British and the Maori in 1840) specifically took indigenous sovereignty away and vested it in the Crown. It marked the start of massive land losses, leaving Maori with 1.6 million hectares of land out of pre-colonial holdings of 25 million. Even so, the Maori have managed to use the treaty to regain some of their rights, for it guaranteed them 'full exclusive and undisturbed possession of their lands and estates, forests, fisheries and other properties'. The Waitangi Tribunal was established in 1975 as a permanent commission of inquiry into Maori claims relating to the treaty. It continues to investigate claims, though it does not settle them – it makes recommendations to the government.

In the US, 371 treaties were signed with Native Americans up to 1871. Numerous legal challenges have followed. There are some parallels with New Zealand/

Fighting back

Aotearoa; for example, the Fort Laramie Treaty of 1868 guaranteed certain rights to Native Americans, including lands being set apart for their exclusive and undisturbed use. Some groups have successfully used this since to try and regain their losses. This treaty, which the defendants fought to present as evidence in court, was a major theme at the trials following the taking of Wounded Knee by members of the American Indian Movement in 1973.[6]

Making a stand

Other kinds of protest have sought to expose injustice and racism generally, using methods that embarrass governments, hold up a mirror to society and take their cue from the American civil rights movement and Black Power. Here are two examples of indigenous Australian activism:

The Freedom Ride

This took place in 1965, when former soccer player and University of Sydney student Charles Perkins decided to expose the high levels of segregation and racism rampant in New South Wales at that time. Perkins and the Reverend Ted Noffs organized a Freedom Ride with 30 white university students from the group Student Action for Aborigines (SAFA). They took a bus to visit the state's most racist country towns. They were pelted with eggs and rotten fruit when they tried to desegregate a swimming pool. The hired bus driver felt so intimidated he quit the tour halfway through. But the resulting publicity raised awareness around the world, exposing Australian racism in the raw. This event set the scene for a pattern of protest that continued and expanded during the 1970s and 1980s, and inspired a whole generation to stand up for their rights. Activist Gary Foley, now Senior Curator of the Indigenous Cultures Program at Museum Victoria in Melbourne, was one of those it inspired. He says of its long-term significance: 'The Freedom Ride represents the beginning of a more radical (and effective) form of protest in the Australian indigenous struggle. A whole new generation of young indigenous political activists were inspired by the Freedom Ride and they went on to form the nucleus of the group that established the Aboriginal Embassy.'

The Aboriginal Embassy

On 26 January 1972, four indigenous activists pitched a beach umbrella on the lawns outside Parliament House, Canberra, and proclaimed the site the 'Aboriginal Embassy'. They declared that a statement made by Prime Minister McMahon the day before – in which he had promised action to review and improve the position of Aboriginal people in Australia – had relegated indigenous people to the status of 'aliens in our own land'. Therefore, as aliens, they had decided to have an embassy of their own. They expected the police swiftly to evict them. But by chance, they had hit on a loophole in the law. There was no law against camping on the lawns of Parliament House so long as there were fewer than 12 tents.

The four – Billy Craigie, Tony Coorey, Michael Anderson and Bert Williams – soon caught the imagination of Australia. Within days they had set up an office tent and a letterbox. Mail began pouring in. Tourist operators saw the site as a new attraction and began bringing busloads of tourists to the 'embassy'. People donated money, brought food and blankets, and invited the 'embassy staff' – now swelled by other activists – home for showers and dinner. The mass media lapped it all up. The Aboriginal Embassy very quickly became the most successful protest venture yet launched by the Aboriginal political movement. The 'embassy' issued a series of demands, which included a call for Aboriginal control of the Northern Territory and minimum compensation of at least Aus\$ 6 billion (US\$ 3.4 billion) and a percentage of the gross national product for alienated lands. Opposition leader Gough

Fighting back

Whitlam paid a formal visit, and declared that a Labor government would reverse McMahon government policies towards Aboriginal people. This was a major breakthrough for the Black Power activists at the core of the protest action.

The tent embassy could not last. The government changed the law and sent nearly 100 police in to arrest the demonstrators. But important points had been made, and the government thoroughly embarrassed. Not least, the televised scenes of over-the-top police violence brought a strong public response. On 30 July more than 2,000 indigenous people and their supporters staged the biggest land rights demonstration in the history of Canberra. There was a government-convened national conference of indigenous representatives, which called for the 'embassy' to be re-established. Next, the Supreme Court declared the Trespass on Commonwealth Lands Ordinance – under which the 'trespassers' had been

---

Folk hero: Eddie Mabo, Australia

Eddie Koiki Mabo (1936-92) was a Torres Strait Islander who fought to challenge unjust white laws. The historic 1992 Mabo Decision by Australia's High Court overturned the notion of terra nullius or no-one's land, which the British had declared when laying claim to the country. The court ruled that the Murray Islanders who had brought the case, led by Eddie, were entitled to possess, occupy, use and enjoy their lands. Unhappily, Eddie did not live to see victory; he had died of cancer a few months earlier. But it was a fitting legacy, and gave hope to others. As a young man, he was exiled from the island as the result of a teenage prank. He got a job on the railways in Townsville, became a spokesperson for fellow laborers from the islands, and began mixing with trade unionists. Later, working as a university gardener, he began attending seminars and reading history and anthropology – especially what white 'experts' had written about his people. He made a key speech at a land rights conference in 1981, and a lawyer suggested bringing a test case. Eddie was chosen to lead the islanders in their action. However, not all indigenous activists call him a hero. Some say the court victory is already tarnished, and see the Mabo Decision as the latest confidence trick to be pulled on black Australians to deny them land rights. ∎

---

evicted – was invalid. The 'embassy' was put up again while the government rushed through more laws. But by now its reputation and credibility on indigenous affairs was in tatters. It lost the next election in a Labor landslide, ending 22 years of conservative rule.

In helping to destabilize the McMahon government, the Aboriginal Embassy protest helped to change the course of Australian history. Activists say its most enduring effect was to influence the moderates in the indigenous struggle. Legendary Sydney Aboriginal community matriarch Shirley Smith has said of her experience: 'If I was going to think of a sign along the road that marked for me the beginning of militant Black Power politics, that sign would have printed on it – Aboriginal Embassy.'7

The Aboriginal Embassy remains in place, though the former shipping container that replaced the original tents as its main office was severely damaged by fire in a suspected arson attack in 2003. Indigenous elders called for a major celebration of 'Sovereignty Day' at the site on 26 January 2012, the 40th anniversary of the first protest there.

Avatar – for real

In *Avatar*, James Cameron's 2009 film, the blue-skinned inhabitants of Pandora, a lushly forested distant moon, have to deal with humans in search of a precious mineral. Though fantasy, the movie's theme rang some familiar bells as the humans sought to infiltrate and sow division among Pandora's inhabitants. In the real world, indigenous people are organizing, using the law and international solidarity, to fight corporate might. Here are a few examples from around the globe.

In **India**, the Dongria Kondh people took on mining giant Vedanta – and won. Responding to vigorous protest, the Indian government's environment ministry denied the London-based company permission to mine in the Nivamgiri Hills, Orissa. Vedanta has lodged a court appeal. However, several shareholders have disinvested a total of $40 million from Vedanta in protest over the company's human rights and environmental record.

In the **Philippines**, the struggle of the Palawan people against the MacroAsia Mining Corporation took a complex twist in June this year when 30 'fake' tribal leaders went to Manila to show support for the company. The main indigenous organization, ALDAW, is accusing both MacroAsia and the national Commission of Indigenous Peoples of using highly manipulative strategies to crush opposition.

The Palawan people are shifting cultivators who survive by growing highland rice. Hundreds of mining applications have been made by companies seeking nickel and chromite from their lands. Open pit and strip mining would devastate the mountains and forests, pollute the rivers and the sea, and destroy the Palawan's burial sites and spiritual places.

In **Nigeria**, after years of denial, Shell finally admitted liability for two massive oil spills that devastated the environment and ruined the livelihoods of the Niger Delta's Ogoni people. Compensation is expected to run into hundreds of millions of dollars.

However, the struggle continues for Ogoni people who are resisting plans to build a military complex on their lands in the Niger Delta. Activists suspect the plans are part of a government drive to further militarize the area in defense of Shell's oil drilling activities.

In **Australia**, Aboriginal people set up road blocks to prevent Woodside Energy starting work on a liquefied natural gas processing plant at James Price Point, Kimberley. The A$30 (US$30.9) billion scheme has divided local aboriginal communities; in May 2011 traditional owners voted 60 per cent in favor of the gas hub. But the vote was taken under threat of compulsory acquisition and many families were excluded from the process, which some say was hijacked by the government of Western Australia. Local artist Charmaine Green is urging fellow indigenous Australians to open their eyes to 'Mr Mining Man' before it's too late. 'I just think the mining companies… have been quite dirty in their tricks, they've been wining and dining

Aboriginal people... they've buttered people up and given them "lollies" to sign on the dotted line.'

In **Malaysia**, a small group of Penan hunter gatherers have scored a victory of sorts over a giant oil palm firm, Shin Yang. The company had been clearing a forest area to which the Penan people were due to be re-settled, to make way for the Murum dam project. But after protests, the Malaysian oil palm giant announced that it was halting work 'pending verification from the authorities' that the land had been designated for the Penan.

The **Republic of Congo** has become one of just two countries in Africa that provides legal protection for its indigenous peoples. The other is the Central African Republic. Congo's new law, passed in February 2011, had been almost seven years in gestation. The country's indigenous people, some of whom are known as Pygmies, constitute one tenth of the population and the law's aim is to counter their chronic marginalization. Currently they are excluded from the education system and lack access to whatever state health services are available. But there are serious gaps in the new law – it does not, for example, include the right to 'free, prior and informed consent' on developments that affect them – a core element of ILO 169 and the UN Declaration on the Rights of Indigenous Peoples.

In **Chile** the Mapuche people are mobilizing to resist the 'legal theft' of their genetic heritage following the Senate's adoption of the International Convention for the Protection of New Plant Varieties (UPOV91), the so-called 'Monsanto Law'. This law would prevent indigenous communities from saving seeds and would threaten their traditional free and collective exchange of plant varieties. Instead indigenous communities will be exposed to the products of corporations like Monsanto, which already holds most of the world's plant species patents. Mapuche poverty will deepen if they become reliant on hybrid or GM seeds and other expensive agricultural products sold by transnationals. Some 150 Mapuche community leaders have signed a declaration against the law.

In **Canada**, three indigenous First Nations – Athabasca Chipewyan, Beaver Lake Cree Nation and Enoch Cree – recently won a Federal Court ruling protecting woodland caribou who are threatened with extinction due to tar sands exploration in Alberta. This is a significant victory in the struggle against the destructive exploration of tar sands on indigenous land and could affect several leases. Despite the efforts by major oil companies such as BP and Petro Canada, a growing number are now joining the indigenous-led opposition to tar sands. For example, 61 First Nations have united to oppose a 1,170 km pipeline that would carry Alberta's tar sands to the west coast.

To find out more about these examples, follow the weblinks in endnote 8 at the end of the chapter.

Fighting back

Intellectual property and biopiracy

Theft of intellectual property, traditional knowledge and biological/genetic resources (biopiracy) has been called a new form of colonization. For one thing, biotechnology companies are busy patenting plant varieties without compensating local farmers, therefore depriving them of the produce of their own sweat. This also involves theft from past generations, since it was they whose lifelong experimentation in the field helped to improve plant varieties. Farmers are banned from planting patented seeds without paying for the 'privilege', and so-called terminator technology has been developed to stop seeds germinating when replanted, which leaves farmers at the mercy of seed producers. All of this threatens local food security and biodiversity, as well as the very survival of small farmers. But the biotechs are not stopping at plants: living beings, micro-organisms, animals and even human cell lines are all being targeted by patent-hunters. Biopiracy has involved extracting the human genes of aboriginal communities that may be useful to science.

The industrialized world, led by the US, is trying to patent increasing numbers of plants and other living things, and it is pushing the South to set up systems for protecting intellectual property rights (IPR) on all inventions. When the World Trade Organization (WTO) adopted the Agreement on Trade Related Aspects of Intellectual Property Rights (TRIPS), the developing countries were given until 2005 to incorporate the granting of patents on inventions into national law, with a later deadline of 2013 for least developed countries.

Part of the trouble with TRIPS is that it fails to protect the genetic resources of the South while allowing genetically modified (GM) materials to be patented. Who controls the GM process? The North, of course.[9] Indigenous peoples and most developing countries hope to tip the balance of control the other way through the Intergovernmental Committee on Intellectual Property and Genetic Resources, Traditional Knowledge and

Folklore. It is hoped that this will become a norm-setting body that develops a binding legal system for protecting all these types of knowledge and resources.[10]

Here is one example, from New Zealand/Aotearoa, of an attempt to stem the tide of theft. The Wai262 Claim to Indigenous Flora and Fauna and Cultural and Intellectual Heritage Rights and Obligations was filed in 1991 with the Waitangi Tribunal, and hearings began in 1997. The claim was brought by Maori concerned about the increasing loss of native plants and animals. It is founded upon the rights guaranteed in Article 2 of the Treaty of Waitangi, cited earlier in this chapter. It is about seeking recognition that *tino rangatiratanga* (the closest word to sovereignty in Maori language) was never given away by Maori, who still have a right to exercise full chiefly authority. The claim includes Maori demands to exercise rights over indigenous flora and fauna, to make decisions about the conservation and control of natural resources, and to take part in and benefit from technological advances to do with breeding, genetic manipulation and other processes connected with the use of fauna and flora.

Maori barrister Maui Solomon represents some of the claimants. He says: 'Maori regard the genetic modification of flora and fauna as the interference or tampering with their *whakapapa* (geneology). Modifying or mixing the genes of the same or different species is analogous to genetic experiments on one's own family members. Whilst this may be regarded by some as emotional blackmail or 'over the top' emotionalism, the issue really boils down to one of respect.' The claim highlights the differences between two opposing world views: one that sees human beings as part of and not dominant over fauna and flora, and one that sees the natural world as ripe for exploitation and domination. In the Maori view, humans are obliged to respect the *mauri* or central life force of every living thing. People's rights to use natural things are balanced by obligations. Maori are not against development, says Maui Solomon. But they do insist that the government, local authorities and commercial companies stop to consider the issues from their cultural perspective.[11]

It took more than 20 years, but the report of the Waitangi Tribunal on Wai262 was finally released in July 2011. It recommended wide-ranging reforms to laws and policies affecting Maori culture and identity and calling for the Crown-Maori relationship to move beyond grievance to a new era based on partnership.

Ko Aotearoa Tēnei ('This is Aotearoa' or 'This is New Zealand') is the Tribunal's first whole-of-government report, addressing the work of more than 20 government departments and agencies.

It is also the first Tribunal report to consider what the Treaty relationship might become after historical grievances are settled, and how that relationship might be shaped by changes in the demographic makeup of New Zealand/Aotearoa over the next 30 to 40 years.

New Zealand, the Tribunal says, is beginning a

transition to a new and unique national identity. But for this transition to succeed, 'Over the next decade or so, the Crown-Maori relationship, still currently fixed on Maori grievances, must shift to a less negative and more future focused relationship at all levels.'

The relationship must change 'from the familiar late-twentieth century partnership built on the notion that the perpetrator's successor must pay the victim's successor for the original colonial sin, into a twenty-first century relationship of mutual advantage in which, through joint and agreed action, both sides end up better off than they were before they started. This is the Treaty of Waitangi beyond grievance.'

The Tribunal said that the Treaty envisages the Crown-Maori relationship as a partnership, in which the Crown is entitled to govern but Maori retain *tino rangatiratanga* (full authority) over their *taonga* (treasures).

Ko Aotearoa Tēnei recommends reform of laws, policies or practices relating to health, education, science, intellectual property, indigenous flora and fauna, resource management, conservation, the Maori language, arts and culture, heritage, and the involvement of Maori in the development of New Zealand's positions on international instruments affecting indigenous rights. These recommendations include law changes and the establishment of new partnership bodies in several of these areas.

These reforms aim to establish genuine partnerships in which Maori interests and those of other New Zealanders are fairly and transparently balanced.[12]

Resistance will also feature in the next chapter, but in a different form: in music. Songs of freedom and struggle have long fired and inspired indigenous movements. Some have also become popular beyond the indigenous world, and entered the mainstream.

1 Peter Matthiessen, *In the Spirit of Crazy Horse*, (London, 1992). **2** With thanks to Charles Swaisland for this information. **3** Taken partly from Andrew Gray, *Indigenous Rights and Development: Self-determination in an Amazonian commu-*

Fighting back

nity, (Berghahn Books 1996), pp9-15. For a brief history of UN relations with indigenous peoples, see UNHCHR Fact Sheet No 9 (Rev. 1) viewable at unhchr.ch/html/menu6/2/fs9.htm **4** IWGIA, *The Indigenous World* 2011. See also the Ogiek website ogiek.org **5** Adapted with permission from Vanessa Baird's report for *New Internationalist* magazine, Oct 2011. **6** See Larry Leventhal, 'Wounded Knee and the 1868 Treaty', *News from Indian Country*, May 1998, viewable at dickshovel.com/lsa12.html **7** An edited version of Gary Foley's account of the Aboriginal Embassy, used with his permission. **8** *Avatar for real weblinks* India: Survival International survivalinternational.org Philippines: No to Mining in Palawan no2mininginpalawan.com Nigeria: Movement for the Survival of the Ogoni People mosop.org nin.tl/noX24e Australia: Save the Kimberley savethekimberley.com nin.tl/o93igs nin.tl/r0vuf0 Malaysia: Rainforest Rescue rainforest-rescue.org Republic of Congo: Rainforest Foundation UK rainforestfoundationuk.org Chile: Mapuexpress mapuexpress.net nin.tl/mRp7Vj Canada: Indigenous Environmental Network ienearth.org/tarsands.html UK Tar Sands Network no-tar-sands.org .
9 From Robert Ali Brac de la Perriere and Franck Seuret, *Brave New Seeds*, (Zed Books 2000). **10** For more information, see iwgia.org; articles on genetic resources and traditional knowledge on the website of the World Intellectual Property Organization, wipo.org, and in *Cultural Survival Quarterly*: culturalsurvival.org/quarterly **11** From 'Intellectual Property Rights and Indigenous Peoples' Rights and Obligations' by Maui Solomon, viewable at inmotionmagazine.com/ra01/ms2.html Additional information supplied direct by the author. **12** waitangi-tribunal.govt.nz/news/media/wai262.asp

6 Music and magic

Music is at the heart of indigenous culture. With other arts, it has helped shape global art forms. Indigenous musicians have enriched World Music, collaborating with others to create highly popular fusions. Songs of resistance drive and inspire rebel movements – and shamans use music and trance dance to work their magic and healing on the world.

MUSIC IS THE FOOD OF LIFE for indigenous communities. It is a vital form of communication, and marks the rites of passage from birth to death. Song is a vehicle for oral history and epic poems that tell of great sorrows, triumphs and other important events in the life of the community. It is used to praise as well as to curse. It appeals to the gods and ancestors, asking for their help in bringing rain and fertility. It inspires the warriors to rout their enemies, and young men and women to woo and win their loved ones. Subversive songs have played a massive role in resistance, when other forms of expression were banned or suppressed.

Some traditional forms

Music and singing are very much part of everyday life, as well as ceremonial occasions. They often accompany story telling, as elders gather round the fire with the younger generation after the day's labor is done. Songs and poetry embody philosophy, beliefs and values. They tell a people's history orally, which is vital in societies where not everyone is literate. They keep threatened languages alive and vibrant. They may be sung by one person, or consist of phrases sung by different people in turn. Unlike Western norms, there is rarely a division between performer and audience. Other people present will sing the chorus, or in some cases urge the singer on by saying something like 'Yes, it is true' at the end of every verse.

Music and magic

Instruments are fashioned from natural materials, or whatever is available. On sacred occasions the Mbuti of Central Africa play a special trumpet, ideally made from the *molimo* tree, though it can also be fashioned from a piece of metal drainpipe. The Baka 'Pygmies' also make instruments from forest materials, and spend hours every day playing them. The music ranges from simple wordless melodies and clapping and rhyme games for children to *likanos*, longer and more complicated tales about myths of origin. Baka instruments include a thin string bow called *limbindi*, and the *ieta* or bow harp. They also make music without instruments – women and children bathing in the river will slap and beat their hands in the water to make polyrhythmic sounds called *liquindi*, or water drumming.

Among Sami people of Lapland the only traditional instrument is the drum, though musicians now use others. The oval single-headed drum is used by shamans to induce trances, and also in divination. The drum dances of the Inuit are played by one or two people on a small oval drum with a wooden frame covered with a bear bladder; they strike the frame instead of the skin. Drums are also central to the music of the Adivasis, or tribal people of India. The Maria (a subgroup) perform a fantastic marriage dance in which boys dance in circles, masked like bisons, accompanied by big cylindrical drums, while the girls dance in a row, beating iron bell-sticks on the ground. In New Guinea, indigenous instruments include the *garamut* or wooden slit drum, which can be anything from one to twelve feet long. Besides making music, it is used to send long-distance signals over land and sea.

Hunters sing about the animals they depend upon. The Mekranoti people of the Amazon sing in a high falsetto as they return from the hunt. From a long way off, villagers can tell who has killed what by the songs they hear. The Mbuti dance before setting off on a hunt – they circle the camp, singing special hunting songs while clapping their hands and leaping about in imitation of the game animals they hope to catch. Hunting songs are broken up into separate notes, each note being sung by one hunter. The *molimo* religious festival is a highpoint in Mbuti life. The men sing songs of praise to the forest, and the *molimo* answers them. (Though referred to as 'the animal of the forest', the *molimo* is actually someone playing a trumpet.) The words are simple and few – often, the Mbuti just sing that 'the forest is good'. But the message is powerful: songs lure the 'animal' to the special *molimo* fire, where dancers swirl in ecstasy through the flames.

Stock-keepers sing to their animals, praising their qualities as if singing about a lover. Praise songs also record warrior exploits, love affairs, great leaders and prophets. Prayer songs address the gods and bless the house, family and animals. Some societies, such as the Maasai, have no instruments besides the human voice, though kudu horns are blown to announce people's arrival at ceremonies such as *eunoto* (where junior warriors upgrade to senior). Australian Aboriginal people learn songs and chants as part of their initiation into adulthood. Each new generation must sing the landscape into being, just as the Dreamtime ancestors did. The traditional music of the Maori, meanwhile, is sung in a way that lies somewhere between speech and song – a style called heightened speech. A leader calls out the main words in a raised pitch and a chorus responds. The rhythm is kept going by vocal sounds and body percussions such as feet stamping, hand clapping and thigh slapping. Maori believe they cannot break the continuity of a song: that invites death or disaster. Chants such as the *patere* often tell the history of the group or describe someone's family tree. Such chants are common right across Oceania, for a person's place in society is very much linked to their family roots.

Music and magic

Music of resistance

From folk music to reggae, the sound of resistance rings out around the world, giving a voice to the oppressed. Rebel music tells alternative stories that challenge the dominant version of events. It records the struggle, and lionizes the heroes of struggle. Some indigenous musicians have even died for their beliefs, and what they represented as music makers. That was the fate of Arnold Ap from West Papua, who founded Mambesak in 1978. The band played songs of freedom, local radio stations loved them, and Mambesak could be heard on battery-powered boom-boxes in the most remote villages. But this was all too much for the government. The Indonesian authorities decided to take action before Ap's renown as a cultural icon got out of hand. The élite military task force, Kopassus, took him into custody in November 1983. He was held without charge for 66 days, then taken by prison guards to a beach where he was shot dead. The authorities claimed he had been trying to escape from prison.[1]

The struggle of the Saharawis of the Western Sahara is one of the most protracted independence struggles today. A whole generation has grown up in exile in refugee camps in the bleakest part of the Algeria desert, ever since Morocco invaded Western Sahara in 1975. The outside world has shown little concern – the UN promised the Saharawis a referendum on self-determination in 1991 but has failed to persuade the Moroccans, who are firmly backed by the French, to allow the referendum to take place. Cultural initiatives have been fundamental to spreading the Saharawi message to the wider world, including a Sahara Film Festival that has been held in the camps annually since 2004. Music has also played its part. The Spanish label NubeNegra first recorded music at a festival in the camps in 1997 and the label has released a number of CDs in the years since, with other releases by Rounder and Sublime Frequencies in the US and by Sandblast in the UK. Among the key Saharawi artists that have emerged in recent years are Mariem Hassan, Leyoad, Nayim Alal, Aziza Brahim, Group Douet and Tiris. Sandblast's description of Tiris's music could serve to describe Saharawi music as a whole: 'Fusing the best of tradition and innovation in a raw and powerful way, they sing of love, loss, and their long struggle and aspirations for independence in their homeland of Western Sahara.'[2]

The Kurds have long used music to keep the fire of cultural identity, and their ambitions for nationhood, burning. For centuries, it has been an important oral vehicle for poetry and history, and connected a scattered people. Kurdish language and literature have been suppressed by ruling regimes in the region. Musicians have been jailed and fled into exile. Until recently, all songs in Kurdish were banned in Turkey and both musicians and listeners were threatened with jail, torture and even death. Everything they sing has to be memorized and passed on orally, often through epic songs. Şivan Perwer is among the most popular Kurdish singers. Often referred to as 'the voice of the Kurdish people', he sings about their longing to be free from persecution. He has been in exile from Turkish Kurdistan for more than 35 years. In 2011, he met Turkey's deputy prime minister in Germany and expressed support for a political solution to the conflict between the government and the Kurdistan Workers' Party (PKK) – which led to his denunciation by the PKK.

On the other side of the world, the story of the late Vincent Lingiari and the fight for Gurindji country has been told in an epic song (see below) by two of Australia's leading songwriters. The words speak for themselves, but it is worth saying something more about this landmark event – the 1966 Gurindji walk-off. The Aboriginal Gurindji community was tired of seeing its land taken and its people used and abused as cheap labor by settlers. One of these exploiters was a Briton, Lord Vestey, who farmed Wave Hill station in the Northern Territory. On 23 August that year, Gurindji leader Vincent Lingiari led his people as well as members of the Ngarinman, Bilinara, Waripiri and Mudpara communities off the station. Vestey offered to raise their wages if they came back, but the strikers refused. They walked on to what they called their new promised land, Daguragu or Wattie Creek, where they held out for nine years. What began as a strike over Aboriginal cattle workers' wages and conditions became something much bigger – the fight to get their land back. Support for the cause came from right across Australia. Victory was a long time coming, but come it did. There has been an annual re-enactment of the walk-off ever since.

From Little Things Big Things Grow

Gather round people let me tell you a story
An eight year-long story of power and pride
British Lord Vestey and Vincent Lingiari
Were opposite men on opposite sides
Vestey was fat with money and muscle
Beef was his business, broad was his door
Vincent was lean and spoke very little
He had no bank balance, hard dirt was his floor…
Gurindji were working for nothing but rations
Where once they had gathered the wealth of the land
Daily the pressure got tighter and tighter
Gurindji decided they must make a stand
They picked up their swags and started off walking
At Wattie Creek they sat themselves down…
Eight years went by, eight long years of waiting
Till one day a tall stranger appeared in the land
And he came with lawyers and he came with great ceremony
And through Vincent's fingers poured a handful of sand
From little things big things grow
From little things big things grow…[3]

Indigenous contributions to World Music

World Music combines the oldest and newest musical forms on earth, from age-old traditions to the latest contemporary fusions. The explosion of World Music over the last two decades has done more than anything else to bring indigenous music and languages to a wider audience. Though purists may abhor fusions, World Music is all about mixing, mingling and borrowing. Spiritual sounds jostle with the music of protest, rap or celebration. Western musicians working with colleagues from the South – in bands such as Afro-Celt Sound System, or the collaborations between 'Britpop' star Damon Albarn and Malian musicians, or Robert Plant's nod towards Tuareg traditions on the *Festival in the Desert* album – have come up with fresh and original combinations to thrill the ear and move the feet. In fact, World Music makes nonsense of some of the arguments around guarding intellectual property – because music has no bounds and musicians have always borrowed from each other. Music is essentially fluid and derivative. If done with respect, musical borrowing brings people together and furthers our understanding of different cultures and histories. Respect must include giving indigenous musicians a fair share of the royalties on collaborative albums.

Many of these musicians create fusions that bridge cultures. They include people who are not themselves indigenous but draw on indigenous musical traditions, as seen below.

Yothu Yindi (meaning 'Mother Child') combine traditional Aboriginal music with modern Western instrumentation. Made up of Aboriginal and non-Aboriginal musicians, this wildly successful Australian band has brought the sound of the outback to the world, as well as promoting the struggle for Aboriginal rights. They aim to unite Australians and all other peoples of the world in peace. Lead singer Mandawuy Wunupingu was Australian of the Year in 1992, and he and fellow band member Witiyana Marika are sons of leaders of the Gumatj and Rirratjingu clans in Northeast Arnhem land, who took part in the Aboriginal land rights movement in the 1960s. Yothu Yindi's music also addresses social injustice and land rights issues, though running through it is the theme of reconciliation between black and white.

Zap Mama is a Belgian-African band who incorporate 'Pygmy' sounds, yodeling and other African and European styles into their unique acapella sound. Congo-born lead singer Marie Daulne got to know 'Pygmy' culture as a child after her Belgian father was killed in a rebellion and her mother took the children into the forests for eight months where 'Pygmies' protected them. The music reflects a mélange of influences, punctuated with all kinds of strange sounds including squeals, laughs and grunts. Daulne sees herself as a kind of global *griotte*, bringing the spiritual powers of the ancestors to the business of healing through harmony.

Mari Boine and her band marry Sami musical traditions and shamanistic beats with modern instrumentation to make what has been called 'vibrant minimalism, rock stripped bare'. She belongs to the radical Nordic school that reworks jazz, rock and traditional music. Mari is influenced both by Christian hymns and traditional *joik*, the improvised singing of the Sami people, and sings in the North Sami language. The *joik* has no formal structure, and can wander about according to the singer's whim. It can be about a person, an animal, a place or whatever the singer fancies. Mari Boine and her band play with the texture and shape of notes, drawing on sounds from other traditions such as Indian, Arabic, Native American and South American.

Senegalese superstars **Youssou N'Dour** and **Baaba Maal** have charmed millions of fans worldwide with their daring mix of indigenous and modern forms. N'Dour was born a *gawlo* or Tukulor (a sub-group of the Fula people) griot on his mother's side. Maal's background is also nomadic Fulani, and he sings in their language, Pulaar. UK-based band **Baka Beyond** mixes Baka sounds from Cameroon with Scottish ballads and

Gypsy fiddling. Malian star **Salif Keita** is inspired by the melodies of Maninka hunters, while fellow Malian **Ali Farka Touré** draws on Songhai and Tuareg musical traditions.

Shamanism

Anthropologists like to remind their students that shamanism, not prostitution, is the world's oldest profession. For centuries, it has been puzzled over and sometimes derided by everyone from skeptical anthropologists to scientists and priests. One French

---

Low thunder on the drum...

Black Elk, an Oglala Sioux, told poet John G Neihardt his life story in the 1930s. It included this description of how, in 1882 when he was just 19, he summoned the spirits to make his first cure. The patient was a sick boy, who recovered.

'Everything was ready now, so I made low thunder on the drum, keeping time as I sent forth a voice. Four times I cried 'Hey-a-a-hey', drumming as I cried to the Spirit of the World, and while I was doing this I could feel the power coming through me from my feet up, and I knew that I could help the sick little boy.

I kept on sending a voice... saying: 'My Grandfather, Great Spirit, you are the only one and to no other can anyone send voices. You have made everything, they say, and you have made it good and beautiful. The four quarters and the two roads crossing each other, you have made. Also you have set a power where the sun goes down. The two-leggeds on earth are in despair. For them, my Grandfather, I send a voice to you... In vision you have taken me to the center of the world and there you have shown me the power to make over... To you and to all your powers and to Mother Earth I send a voice for help.'

[He then sings 'to the source of all life'.]

'While I was singing this I could feel something queer all through my body, something that made me want to cry for all unhappy things, and there were tears on my face. Now I walked to the quarter of the west, where I lit the pipe, offered it to the powers, and, after I had taken a whiff of smoke, I passed it around. When I looked at the sick little boy again, he smiled at me, and I could feel that the power was getting stronger.'

John G Niehardt, *Black Elk Speaks: being the life story of a holy man of the Oglala Sioux* Morrow, 1932.

---

priest, after seeing shamans at work in Brazil, called them 'ministers of the devil'. Anthropologist Claude Lévi-Strauss likened them to psychoanalysts. Today, their knowledge is better understood and admired, and their healing powers are legendary.

Shamans, who can be male or female, mediate between human beings and the spirit world. They communicate with spirits and may be possessed by them. Their powers include divination, prophecy, healing, and charming animals in order to make them docile to hunt. They are fundamentally ambivalent; in order to cure people, they must also have the power to harm them. Some drink bitter substances like bark teas and vomit them up before they can make contact with the spirits. Others use hallucinogenic drugs. Powerful dreams convey many insights. Many shamans use drumming, singing and dancing to induce states of ecstasy and trance.

Here are two examples showing how shamanism is practiced in different parts of the world. There are many other forms it can take.

Siberian shamanism

This is probably the oldest form of spiritual healing in the world. It began in prehistoric times, and spread through China to the south and north. Chinese shamans invented and developed acupuncture and other healing practices. In the north, it spread over the Bering Strait into America, where shamans became the medicine people of the Native Americans. In Siberia, it nearly died out altogether under Stalin. Shamans were killed, or sent to the Gulag camps, and shamanism went underground for years.

Customarily, Siberian shamans deal with everything from illness to expelling bad spirits from people's homes and finding lost animals. They do not guarantee success in every case. They work by interceding between people and the spirit world. They heal by directing and sometimes deflecting spiritual energy, and usually go into a light trance (or sometimes a deep one) during a healing session.

They use many techniques, including the laying on of hands, and use drums as a vehicle to help them on their way. Patients talk of feeling energy moving round their bodies while they are being treated. Siberian shamanism is not an exact science or practice; each shaman has his or her own way of doing things. They also have their own specialties, such as healing children, or being good at extra-sensory perception.[4]

Shamanism among San people

From the evidence of rock paintings found right across southern Africa, archeologists claim a long history of the San's shamanic, transformative trance dance ritual. The dance is exceptional among indigenous shamanic rituals because the healers work indiscriminately with all who have gathered – including foreign researchers and tourists. This way of working is considered a distinctive example of the San's co-operative egalitarian behavior.

Typically – a hard word to use among people known for their flexibility – the dance consists of women sitting together in a tight semi-circle around a fire, singing a repetitive simple song and rhythmically clapping their hands. In the center a healer, or healers, usually men, dance in a shuffling and stamping manner. Using the energy of the women the healer seeks to tap into a healing energy, called n|om in one of the San languages, Ju| 'hoansi. If all works well they feel a build-up of energy in their abdomen and chest as they dance. The process is painful and is often said to be like dying. If the energy builds up enough the healer can 'see' what is wrong with people. Having identified where the sickness is, the healer then rubs the afflicted area of the person's body. This draws the sickness into his own body; the healer must then expel the sickness out through the top of his head or the bottom of his neck.

Different San peoples describe what they do and

see during 'trance' healing in different ways. General themes involve the healer climbing up a thread from his body to the home of god or the devil (not that the San call it this – generally, they do not believe in a fully evil being) where he must plead for the life of the sick person. Sometimes healers say they change into lions or ride away into the night on the backs of eland or other animals. When they change shape, healers are often described as undergoing transformation. Similarly the dance ritual is often regarded as a transformative process in which differences, sickness, problems and anger can be reconciled and life thereby remains a possibility in a testing social and physical environment.[5]

But not even the shamans can prevent some of the major challenges facing indigenous peoples. The final chapter looks at some of these challenges in the light of 'development' and tries to offer some conclusions.

1 Adapted from Eben Kirksey, 'Playing up the primitive', *New Internationalist* No 344, and personal communication. **2** The quote is from *The Rough Guide to World Music* Vol 1, p 565. Much of this section draws, with the publishers' permission, from the two-volume *Rough Guide to World Music*, edited by Simon Broughton, Mark Ellingham and Richard Trillo (Rough Guides 2000). **3** Edit of *From Little Things Big Things Grow* by Paul Kelly and Kev Carmody. Information taken from lingiari. startyourweb.com **4** With thanks to Ken Hyder, journalist, musician and shaman, for supplying this information. **5** Thanks to Chris Low for writing this contribution.

7 Development, justice and future challenges

Change is afoot for indigenous peoples. After decades in which development schemes aimed at helping indigenous peoples have often done more harm than good, communities are now taking more control of their own development and are speaking for themselves. What are the key challenges and future ways forward?

THERE'S SOMETHING IN the air. After decades of wrangling, much of the world in 2007 signed up to a UN Declaration on the Rights of Indigenous Peoples, supporting their centuries-long struggle to recover their lands, dignity and autonomy. In Australia, the word 'sorry' finally passed the lips of a prime minister in 2008, officially recognizing that stealing a generation of Aboriginal children from their parents was wrong. In Washington, also in 2008, the World Bank was shamed by Congolese Pygmies, who proved that the institution was breaking its own rules by helping logging companies destroy their country's rainforest, the world's second lung. In Bolivia, indigenous leader Evo Morales has been president of the country since 2006, presiding over a program of radical change that has indigenous values at its heart.

After centuries of their rights being trampled upon and their interests being disregarded, over the last decade indigenous peoples worldwide have increased their level of resistance – and their voices have arguably been heard more clearly than ever before. Peoples who were previously routinely seen as 'obstacles to development' have increasingly been recognized as allies of the global justice movement – and have been claimed by some to be in the vanguard of opposition to an economic and

Call of the wild

Here's a confrontation that rarely hits the news headlines – yet it has profound ramifications for all of us.

On one side are people who live in the wild places in the world – the forests, the highlands, the plains. They are indigenous people who, according to Western standards and norms, are the poorest and most isolated but who see themselves as the guardians of nature.

On the other are people who occupy the wild places of capitalism, the boardrooms of major corporations and the governments that support them. Foremost among them are the big industries – energy, mining, banking – that see themselves as the guardians of growth and consumerism.

The fight is over nothing less than the natural world we inhabit and our capacity to survive global warming. With each day this clash is becoming more pertinent and intense.

Consumer demand – today coming equally from China and Brazil, as well as the more traditional places – is spurring companies to penetrate the most remote regions of the world in their quest for more and yet more minerals, timber, oil and other energy sources. The current rise in commodity prices is cream on their profit cake.

Indigenous people know what happens when their land is invaded; when their forests and waterways become denuded or polluted. They are organizing and fighting back.

Unlikely as it may seem, indigenous people are at the forefront of the struggle to save the planet. Their courage and their worldview can inspire those of us who don't think life on earth should be determined by the boardroom bottom line. We, in our turn, have a role to play in defending the defenders.

Vanessa Baird, *New Internationalist*, October 2011.

social model based upon the rapacious exploitation of the planet's resources.

Breakthroughs at the United Nations

The new millennium brought a new breakthrough for indigenous peoples in terms of their acknowledgment by the United Nations. In December 2000 a Permanent Forum on Indigenous Issues was finally created, officially drawing the representatives of indigenous peoples into the UN system for the first time.

To most people this was a major breakthrough,

though some have taken a more cynical view. Rudolph C Rÿser, chair and executive director of the Center for World Indigenous Studies, has written: 'The Indigenous Peoples' Forum is a hoax played upon indigenous peoples. The central question raised by advocates of the Forum is not whether the Forum can actually represent specific concerns and interests of indigenous nations or do anything about those concerns – they want to know whether they will personally be appointed to [it].'[1]

He pointed out that membership of the Forum will be determined by representatives of governments, not by indigenous peoples. Indigenous groups worked hard to ensure that they would in fact control the nomination of the eight indigenous experts on the Forum. Indigenous peoples demanded that the Forum must have its own secretariat, staffed by indigenous persons, instead of coming under the UN's Economic and Social Council (ECOSOC). Its first chairperson, Ole Henrik Magga, welcomed it for enabling 'people who have been left out in the cold and dark to come into a warm well-lighted house to discuss things that mattered to them'. This wrangling over the Forum has since been overshadowed by an even more significant breakthrough at the UN.

The adoption of the UN Declaration on the Rights of Indigenous Peoples by the UN General Assembly in September 2007 – after decades of wrangling – was an even more momentous event. While even this landmark moment seemed at first to be sullied by four major countries voting against its adoption – Australia, Canada, New Zealand and the US, all of which have significant indigenous populations – over the years that followed, even this tarnishing was rubbed clean.

According to the International Work Group for Indigenous Affairs (IWGIA), 'Australia revised its position in 2009, officially endorsing the Declaration. In 2010, New Zealand, Canada and the US followed suit. Furthermore, two countries that had previously abstained from the vote also expressed their commitment to the Declaration. These are important developments and the value of the consensus around the Declaration cannot be underestimated. The Declaration is truly a universal instrument protecting the rights of indigenous peoples… [Notwithstanding this, there are] concerns regarding the conditionality of New Zealand, Canada and the US's endorsement of the Declaration. All three countries have set the Declaration within the limits of their existing legal and constitutional framework, despite strong encouragement from indigenous peoples and civil society to make an unqualified endorsement. It also needs to be noted that a number of countries that abstained from the vote in 2007 have not begun a process of reconsideration, despite the serious human rights situation of the indigenous peoples in these countries. These include, for example, the Russian Federation, Bangladesh and Burundi, to name but a few.

'One of the key elements of the Declaration is the acknowledgment of indigenous peoples' right to free, prior and informed consent (FPIC) as a key principle and instrument with which to assert their right to self-determination. FPIC has been seen by many states as a contentious issue, as it could obstruct their countries' development. However, the current reality is that development is obstructing the lives of indigenous peoples. Development aggression in the form of logging, plantations, mega-dams and other land development projects continues to be the major challenge facing indigenous peoples. Many development projects still go ahead without states having fulfilled their duty to obtain FPIC from the indigenous peoples affected. This is, for example, the case in Malaysia, Peru and Brazil, where large dams flood indigenous lands without the indigenous peoples having been consulted or their free, prior and informed consent obtained. In Nepal, 2010 started with a nationwide strike on the part of the indigenous peoples demanding the establishment of a mechanism in the Constituent Assembly to implement the principle of FPIC. This failure to implement prior consultation has also been at the root of social protest in Ecuador, Bolivia and Guatemala.'[2]

Development: good or bad?

Over the centuries, indigenous peoples have suffered a great deal at the hands of those who sought to 'develop' them. Colonizers, missionaries, anthropologists, governments and aid agencies – they have all had a go. Some had the best will in the world, some had the worst. Either way, it was usually misplaced because indigenous peoples did not tend to ask for it. It was (and still is) often driven by racism and the belief that indigenous peoples were backward, and therefore obstacles to national development.

Now they demand the right to develop on their own terms and at their own pace. Some groups have created a model for change that builds on their traditional self-reliance. Some have been able to develop and strengthen their negotiating power with the state, and with outsiders who try to exploit them. These models are useful for others to follow. Sensitive governments, aid agencies and human rights organizations would do well to listen and learn. Equally, though indigenous peoples have the right to refuse contact, there are strong arguments for their being open to forging useful alliances with outside organizations, and lobbying alongside others. For some say it is the 'separateness' of indigenous peoples that has placed them so much at risk, together with their uneasy relationship with national society. Those who argue that they are best left that way – remote, untouched and untainted by the modern

> 'Don't mistake us. We are not a backward-looking people. Like others we want development and we want to improve our lives and the lives of the next generations... But we want to control this development in our land and over our lives. And we demand a share both in decision-making and in the benefits of development.'
>
> *Unnamed indigenous person, the Philippines.*

Development, justice and future challenges

'The government talks about development. Let it help us with water, then leave us to our own place. We can think for ourselves; we can think about what we need.'

Mogetse Kaboikanyo, Kgalagadi man, Botswana. Quoted in Survival appeal on behalf of the San, August 2002. Kaboikanyo, who was in his fifties, died shortly after being evicted by the Botswana government from the Central Kalahari Game Reserve.

world – may be condemning them to extinction. Isolation can deprive indigenous peoples of the skills and knowledge they need to defend themselves; otherwise they risk seeing more of their rights and land eroded. Also, seeking legal redress for injustice at courts in the Western world may lead to better outcomes: the compensation is bigger, there is less likelihood of local bigwigs and corrupt politicians intervening, and the media coverage is sure to raise awareness of your story all around the world.[1] This is one of the potential payoffs of North-South alliances, on this and other social justice issues. On the other hand, indigenous peoples who choose to remain isolated have every right to do so, and must have their land and other rights respected regardless of their relationship with wider society and the state.

Nonetheless, most people would agree that the modern world cannot be kept at bay indefinitely. The challenge for development workers and indigenous groups is 'how to exploit the useful features of modern society without alienation and suffering'.[3] This is what two young San people, one from South Africa and the other from Namibia, have to say about the kind of development the San want, which seeks to strike a balance between upholding 'traditional' culture while using what the outside world can offer. Both of them are involved with the Working Group of Indigenous Minorities in Southern Africa, established by

'I hope we can get to the point where we don't have to be frozen images of the past.'

Sandra Sunrising Osawa, Makah filmmaker, US.

the San in 1996 as an umbrella organization to enable their widely scattered communities to communicate with each other and to represent the San nationally and internationally.

'Bad development' globally has included:

- forced assimilation of indigenous peoples into national society
- forced urbanization and resettlement schemes
- forced removals and relocation
- national development projects created at indigenous peoples' expense, for example by building highways and hydroelectric projects, or allowing such things as mining, oilfields and commercial hunting on indigenous land
- promoting strong ethnic groups over weaker ones

San want development at their own pace

'WIMSA believes that San communities themselves should find ways to be involved in development. Rather than wait for governments to act, they should initiate self-development programs – with children, youth, parents and elders, or all age groups together so the rich culture and traditions are imparted to new generations. We need the freedom to implement our self-development projects at our own pace. Experience has taught us to keep projects simple so they are sustainable. We now see San groups in Namibia, Botswana and South Africa setting up income-generating projects such as tourist campsites and craft shops, and establishing San kindergartens where community members tell traditional stories and teach tracking skills and traditional games.

'As for assistance from outside, we need to build our capacity, learn how to organize ourselves and make longer-term plans. We need assistance with training, especially in bookkeeping, computer operating, marketing, catering, agriculture, tourism and entrepreneurship. We hope governments and NGOs will assist us with training. We also hope for opportunities to participate in meetings that enable us to network with other indigenous groups. We need schools where young children are taught in their mother tongue, and human rights and HIV/AIDS awareness programs in our own languages. Most of all we need land. Our ancestral lands were all lost to colonial powers and dominant ethnic groups. Without land we have no culture, no traditions, no livelihood.'[4] ■

San denied rights despite court ruling, Botswana

On 13 December 2006, the Botswana High Court ruled in favor of the 2,000 San indigenous people in the case they had brought about their relocation from their traditional lands in what is now the Central Kalahari Game Reserve. Judges gave the former occupants of the Reserve the right to return, as well as to hunt, but government officials have since continued to prevent people from moving back and have arrested those caught hunting within the Reserve. Those San people who are trying to eke out a living on the reserve are struggling due to lack of water and social services denied them by the government.

IWGIA - The Indigenous World 2011

- supporting men and ignoring women
- ignoring children's rights
- giving control of wildlife and 'conservation' to Western-driven bodies
- introducing inappropriate technology
- forcing religious, political or other alien ideologies upon people.

Flawed development schemes include both top-down mega-projects (those imposed from on high) and smaller community projects. What indigenous peoples want is bottom-up alternatives (those arising from the grassroots) to the discredited top-down models, that recognize their human rights, particularly their collective rights to land, natural resources and a healthy environment of their choosing. Indigenous peoples also want empowerment in the form of information, pros and cons, so that they are able to make informed decisions.

When 'bad development' goes wrong, indigenous peoples and the environment pay dearly. Some ill-thought out schemes have wrecked the latter. Many indigenous territories contain high levels of biological diversity, and provide vital water catchment functions for large geographic regions. When this ecosystem is disrupted, it not only affects indigenous communities but wider non-indigenous irrigation and

Arundhati Roy on India's war against its indigenous people

The campaigner and novelist Arundhati Roy has dedicated much of her recent writing and interviews to highlighting the plight of indigenous people in central India on whom the Indian army is waging war.

'Those resisting their impoverishment are being labeled "terrorists" – and these are not just the Maoist rebels who have taken to arms, but others who are involved in unarmed, but militant, struggles against the government. A climate has been created which criminalizes dissent of all kinds.

'There are hundreds, maybe even thousands of the poorest people in jails across the country under charges of sedition and waging war against the state. Many others are just charged under the common criminal penal code. There are the other 'seditionists' too, of course – those who have been fighting for self-determination after being inducted into the Union of India without their consent when the British left in 1947. I refer to Kashmir, Manipur, Nagaland… in these places, tens of thousands have been killed, hundreds of thousands tortured in the nightmarish interrogation centers and army camps all around the country. And now, the Indian army is migrating to the heart of the country – to fight the Adivasi people whose lands the corporations covet. They say Pakistan is a military dictatorship, but I don't think the Pakistani army has been actively deployed against its 'own' people the way the Indian army has been: Kashmir, Manipur, Nagaland, Hyderabad, Goa, Telengana, Punjab and now, Chhattisgarh, Jharkhand, Orissa…

'The 2G scam [in which the Indian government sold off mobile phone licenses on the cheap to private companies which then sold on the licenses for huge profits that were lost to the public exchequer] enraged the Indian middle classes, who saw it as a betrayal, as a moral problem, not a systemic or structural one. Somehow, the fact that the government has signed hundreds of secret Memorandums of Understanding (MOUs) privatizing water, minerals and infrastructure, and signing over forests, mountains and rivers to private corporations, does not seem to generate the same outrage. Unlike in the 2G scam, these secret MOUs do not have just a monetary cost, but human and environmental costs that are devastating. They displace millions of people and wreck whole ecosystems. The mining corporations pay the government just a tiny royalty and rake in huge profits. Yet the people who are fighting these battles are being called terrorists and terrorist sympathizers. Even if there were no corruption and everything were above board on these deals, it would be daylight robbery on an unimaginable scale.'

Arundhati Roy, interviewed in *New Internationalist* 445, September 2011.

> 'Stop all logging activities… Give back to us what is properly ours. Save our lives, have respect for our culture.'
>
> *1987 declaration by the Penan people of Borneo.*

farming systems that rely upon its water supplies and other resources. Some development schemes have also upset relationships between men and women, usually at the expense of women – by taking away women's land and resource rights and undermining their role as producers and traders. Others have stoked up tensions and rivalries between indigenous and other communities, leading to bloodshed. Food aid has created dependency. Concentrating wells, bore-holes, schools, churches and clinics in one place has led to bloated townships where newly sedentarized nomads scrap over meager resources – and women despair because their unemployed men have taken to drink.

So what should responsible governments, NGOs and other development actors do? They must beware of imposing any ideology, however worthy. An intervention that involves political action can backfire, triggering reprisals for the indigenous group concerned. Where several NGOs compete for influence over a particular indigenous group, as has happened in the Amazon, there can be dire effects for the supposed beneficiaries. Other pitfalls to avoid include paternalism, ethnocentric attitudes, ignoring indigenous skills and indigenous knowledge, giving hand-outs, only supporting indigenous groups who are well-organized and can help themselves (because that is easier), using dubious power brokers, and being in too much of a hurry. Outside agencies must avoid top-down strategies.

'Good development' includes providing resources for the self-management of projects, enabling indigenous groups to gain political

> 'I believe in our fight for sovereignty and I believe if we are to accept anything less then we will be selling ourselves short.'
>
> *Darlene Mansell, Aboriginal woman, Australia.*

and legal representation and secure land and resource rights. It also includes:

- Encouraging consensus, and urging people to transcend traditional divisions in order to present a united front
- Meeting real needs
- Helping to restore confidence, and allowing plenty of time
- Building consultation and participation into all development work
- Showing respect
- Identifying priorities instead of trying to solve all problems at once
- Supporting women's and children's rights and development
- Providing mobile services for nomads (clinics, schools, 'barefoot doctors' and vets)
- Providing literacy, numeracy, management, rights and advocacy training.

There are plenty of examples of good practice. Among these is the training that Anti-Slavery, Franciscans International and Trócaire did for partner organizations on how to use the UN's International Labour Organization (ILO) mechanisms to combat trafficking and bonded labor.[5] First Peoples Worldwide is working with local partners on a new project called 'Speaking Up', which aims to improve the capacity of indigenous communities to address the threats they face from the extractive resource industry. In a US-Africa collaboration, Africans are being trained to use indigenous knowledge for conflict resolution/management on their continent,[6] while the Forest Peoples Programme has produced a toolkit on indigenous women's

> 'We recognize that the fight is a long one and we cannot hope to win it alone. To win, to secure the future, we must join hands with like-minded people and create strength through unity.'
>
> *The Haudenosaunee Declaration of the Iroquois, US.*

rights and the African human rights system.[7]

> 'I just want to wander in freedom in my country.'
>
> *Unnamed Tuareg woman, Burkina Faso.*

Bad development is not, of course, only caused by NGOs. The World Bank, state governments and private corporations have run riot over indigenous territories with their dams, roads, mines, logging, oil and gas extraction and other schemes – often carried out in the name of 'progress' and national development. For example, the US company PT Freeport has devastated the central highlands of West Papua with its gold and copper mining operations. It has even cut the top off one mountain, believed by the indigenous Amungme people to be the sacred head of their mother; the Amungme see Freeport now dipping into her heart. Freeport plans to increase its dumping of untreated tailings into the Aghawaghon River system to 285,000 tons daily – the equivalent of a ten-ton truckload every three seconds. Indigenous people have not only seen their environment trashed, but have also died and suffered at the hands of the Indonesian military, which has provided 'security' for Freeport throughout its 42-year presence in West Papua.[6]

Landmark Endorois case, Kenya

On 4 February 2010, the African Commission on Human and Peoples' Rights ruled on the Endorois case, condemning the Kenyan government's expulsion of the Endorois people from their ancestral lands in the 1970s and ordering the government to restore the Endorois' rights to their ancestral lands and to compensate them. This is a landmark ruling as it is the first to determine who indigenous peoples in Africa are, and what their rights to land are. The Endorois decision is a victory for all indigenous peoples across Africa. The case is an historic milestone in the struggle for recognition of indigenous peoples' rights to land and sets an unprecedented reference. However, the Commission has no powers to enforce the ruling; it remains to be seen whether the Kenyan government will uphold it.

All but the last sentence from IWGIA – The Indigenous World 2011

Breakthrough Cree agreement, Canada

Below, Romeo Saganash, lawyer and spokesperson for the Cree Council of the Cree Nation talks about their agreement.

'It's hard to make dispossession of lands compatible with human rights, no matter how long ago it took place. Indigenous peoples can only survive and prosper if they can use their lands; that is fundamental.

In February 2002, a breakthrough agreement was signed between the Cree Nation and the government of Quebec which could be the basis for a rights-based approach elsewhere in the world. They are the only government to recognize the mutually beneficial nature of an understanding with indigenous peoples based on co-operation, partnership and mutual respect. Before, development on our lands mostly benefited others. Land laws were based on the erroneous idea that indigenous people could not manage the land economically, which forced us into a position of dependency on the government and a life on the edge of poverty. Now, the Cree will be responsible for their own development and economy, and will benefit directly from development. The agreement includes a new forestry regime that will involve consultation with the Cree, the cancellation of a controversial hydro-electric project on Cree land, more Cree involvement in mining that will lead to more jobs for Cree, and the establishment of a Cree Development Corporation. Unusually, this agreement is not based on damages but makes the Cree part of the official development process. This disturbs some people, including some Cree who have become used to the idea of indigenous peoples being opposed to governments and development. The Quebec government and the Cree have bravely abandoned the old oppositional positions.'[8] ∎

Voices and choices: indigenous peoples and aid

Mike Sansom of African Initiatives outlines some lessons and challenges (below). African Initiatives is a social justice organization that promotes the rights of all people fully to participate in the social, political and economic decisions that affect their lives at a community, national and international level. It supports communities and their organizations in Africa by providing resources, training, advice and advocacy.

In a world where people often profess utopian ideals of egalitarianism and sharing natural resources for the common good, it is a sad irony that those communities which come nearest to attaining that dream are in danger of being wiped out.

All indigenous peoples have their own social structures and organization. Yet most non-governmental organizations (NGOs) encourage them to set up new organizations, which invariably represent Western hierarchical models, and subsequently fail. While NGOs proclaim cultural sensitivity, many seem to deny or ignore the legitimacy of traditional social, political and economic systems. NGOs also tend to claim that they are committed to participatory approaches to working with communities – yet they often miss or avoid the priority issues. The primary threat to indigenous peoples is the loss of their land, yet most development agencies continue to focus on service delivery.

Conservation is a major threat to indigenous peoples all over Africa. Hunter-gatherers face extinction, and have been banned from carrying bows and arrows while seeing their lands turned into commercial hunting blocks, which some conservationists regard as legitimate land use. To my knowledge no major NGO is challenging the methods and legitimacy of conservation organizations. The major conservation NGOs are actually strengthening government departments that promote this approach.

If Shell Oil or a government were alienating people from vast tracts of land there would be an NGO outcry. One example is Serengeti National Park in Tanzania. Serengeti, the size of Northern Ireland, has been denied to pastoralists for over a generation. So why do the major development NGOs mimic the three monkeys – hear no evil, see no evil, speak no evil – when conservation bodies contribute to the marginalization and impoverishment of indigenous peoples, and in some cases threaten their very survival?

If they are to survive, indigenous peoples need security of land, appropriate education and self-representation. With these, they will be better equipped to determine their own destiny. Education will enable them to expand their world view, understand their place in the world and adapt their mode of production by acquiring new skills. If they choose to retain traditional modes such as pastoralism, it will be done from an informed and secure base.

This should be the focus of development interventions; unfortunately, it is not. Northern development and rights organizations (some do make a distinction) are often disempowering, taking away the right of indigenous peoples to tell their own story and represent themselves. If the emphasis is on service delivery (funding healthcare, education, water supplies and other basic services) this can unwittingly undermine local culture with zero or negative impacts.

In our experience, taking land cases to court is rarely successful, puts resources and control in the hands of lawyers and NGOs, and increases tension between governments and indigenous peoples. Likewise high profile campaigns in the North done 'on behalf of' indigenous peoples are not accountable to affected communities, can have negative consequences and reinforce the patronizing myth that indigenous peoples cannot represent themselves.

Community advocacy

An alternative approach is community advocacy. This involves recognizing and building on the legitimacy of indigenous peoples' social processes. Instead of doing advocacy 'on behalf of' people, communities control their own representation. Community advocacy also includes research, documentation and, crucially, analysis of their situation. It is a social process that starts at community level, and enables people to make clear links between their micro-political situation and the macro one. For example, providing a Tanzanian pastoralist organization with information on debt and structural adjustment enabled them to analyze the forces and interests behind their eviction from traditional lands in the name of conservation.

Northern NGOs have to be careful not to dominate the debate around globalization, denying the space to indigenous *peoples in particular to develop their own critiques, analyses of how they fit into the world and strategies for influencing it. Strengthening the voices of marginalized peoples is the beginning of democratization and global justice. Community advocacy gives a voice and choice to indigenous peoples and has the potential to fundamentally challenge the inequities of economic globalization.*

What lies ahead

Self-development and self-determination are the key words. These drive the indigenous movement, and all who wish to support it. The right to self-determination is a fundamental principle of human rights law, and represents the individual and collective right of people (not simply governments) to freely determine their political status and pursue economic, social and cultural development. The principle is linked to the decolonization process that followed the UN Charter of 1945, in which self-determination featured strongly. Two important UN studies concluded that people have a right to self-determination if they have a history of independence or self-rule in an identifiable territory, a distinct culture, and a will and capability to regain self-government. However, many indigenous peoples failed to gain from decolonization because it did not restore sovereignty or full governance. Very often, colonial powers relinquished control to one group of people in a contested territory, leaving other groups out in the cold. Colonization has even continued in some places; one example is Tibet, seized by China in 1949-50

'We will not accept any cosmetic solution short of total and complete national independence… East Timor will be free, independent and sovereign.'

Roque Rodriques of FRETILIN, the liberation movement of East Timor, in 1979.

'We don't want power over white institutions; we want white institutions to disappear. That's revolution.'

Russell Means, Native American activist.

and occupied ever since. The problem now is that the international community has largely ignored indigenous peoples' call for recognition of their right to self-determination, dismissing it as political rhetoric.[9]

Some communities are striving for complete territorial autonomy, self-government and recognition of sovereignty. Realistically, they are unlikely to achieve full sovereignty in today's world of nation states, and none have so far done so. Most indigenous peoples claim that they have never given up their sovereignty, and accuse nation states of violating it on a daily basis. Others may settle for running some of their own affairs, controlling local political institutions and revenues from such money-spinners as tourism and mining on their land. Either way, there are potential snags. Self-determination rarely guarantees indigenous peoples complete freedom from oppression or full recognition of their rights. Self-interested leaders may feel it gives them the right to do what they like, at the expense of weaker sections of the community – such as women, youngsters or disabled people. Power may become concentrated in fewer hands, and some people may interpret self-management as the right to claim funds while denying accountability.

Unfortunately there have been cases of indigenous NGOs becoming dependent on handouts, and failing to account for these to their own communities. When there is big money to be had, indigenous leaders (and any other leaders for that matter) can sometimes become more oriented to international donors than their own people. There is also a danger of indigenous élites in multi-ethnic societies dominating the development agenda at the expense of other marginalized ethnic groups. By representing itself as indigenous, thereby making itself more eligible for donor funding, a group may aggrandize itself over others in the same area – driving a wedge between one community and its neighbors. These are uncomfortable truths, by no means universal, which should be aired and discussed nonetheless. How can such problems be overcome? There may be lessons to be learned from longer-established social movements such as the women's movement, the environmental movement,

---

Lakota 'divorce' the US

In December 2007, a delegation from the Lakota Freedom Movement announced that their nation was pulling out of all treaties signed with the US government and was declaring independence. The new country, simply named Lakotah, would issue its own passports to anyone who wished to become a citizen – including non-natives – the only requirement being that they given up their US citizenship. The country would be tax free, its political structure decentralized, and its borders would extend to the Lakota (Sioux) nation's pre-treaty territory, encompassing swathes of North and South Dakota, Montana, Wyoming and Nebraska. The 'face' of the independence movement is Russell Means, the controversial Sioux activist-cum-Hollywood actor with a reputation for dramatizing native desire for self-determination. According to Means: 'In the 20th century we tried armed struggle again. It didn't work. We tried protesting. We tried petitioning. We tried voting for democrats. We tried the courts. We tried every way imaginable to try to get some kind of redress. We are at risk of disappearing as a people... The colonial apartheid system does not work for us.'

The extent of Lakota support for the initiative remains unclear. The US Bureau of Indian Affairs commented that the group's withdrawal 'doesn't mean anything'.

Shane Bauer, *New Internationalist* 410, April 2008.

gay rights, the American civil rights movement and Black Power. Though widely divergent in many ways, they faced similar challenges at certain points in their history around power imbalances, internal dissent and funding.

In the scramble for rights, and UN recognition, there is a danger of privileging one ethnic group over another, leading to jealousies, inequalities and trampled rights. Is it fair that Nuer people are considered to be indigenous, but not Kikuyu? Maasai, but not the Ndebele? The Indigenous Peoples of Africa Coordinating Committee (IPACC) suggests there is no contradiction: 'All Africans should enjoy full and equal rights. There are principles about collective rights in the UN Draft Declaration that could be usefully applied in Africa, beyond the claims of indigenous peoples. This does not negate the importance of using the UN process to challenge the systematic discrimination against peoples' aboriginal identities and their continued use of ancient territories, economic and cultural practices.' In Africa, it says, 'it is the maintenance of systematic inequality and marginalization that defines who is indigenous today'.[10]

But this remains a difficult issue. There is a tightrope to be walked between showing due reverence for marginalized peoples, ethnic reification (and the hardening of ethnic boundaries that goes with that) and acknowledging the genuine needs and rights of particular communities. Indigenous and tribal peoples should remember that they are themselves the product of colonial attempts to 'fix' ethnic identity. In fact, tribes and tribal identities are and were always fluid. We need to keep a sense of perspective and a good grasp of history.

Indigenous politics and the rise of Evo Morales

The last decade has been a remarkable time for indigenous peoples not just because of greater recognition – the emergence of the UN Declaration and victories in key court battles – but also because they have been gaining more political power and influence. The most significant development in this direction has been the access to power of Evo Morales, who became President of Bolivia in 2006. An Aymara, he worked, like his parents, as a coca farmer and eventually became leader of the coca growers' trade union, achieving notice for his resistance to US attempts to eradicate the coca crop in Chapare province. As leader of the Movement for Socialism party (MAS), he contested the 2005 presidential election and came tantalizingly close to winning it, in the end being pipped to the post by millionaire entrepreneur Gonzalo Sanchez de Lozada. His victory as Bolivia's first-ever indigenous president in the election in December 2005 sent shockwaves around the world and he embarked upon a radical program, using the army to nationalize the country's oil and gas fields. Over the next two years the minimum wage was raised twice and oil and gas revenues were used to provide a small annual grant for each child in education, free healthcare for children and a universal old-age pension. Morales has maintained a close relationship with other left-orientated leaders in Latin America such as Fidel and Raúl Castro in Cuba and Hugo Chávez in Venezuela.

More striking even than his socialism in a world dominated by free-market globalization, however, has been his self-identification as indigenous and the impact this has had on his approach to environmental issues. In 2009 a new Bolivian constitution was approved in a referendum, defining the country as a 'plurinational' state and enshrining the idea of autonomy not just for provinces but also for indigenous groups. Later in 2009 he was re-elected as president by a landslide and was declared a 'World Hero of Mother Earth' by the UN General Assembly.

His profound dissatisfaction with the official negotiations over climate change at the Copenhagen conference in December 2009 led him to convene an alternative conference in Bolivia in 2010, the World People's Conference on Climate Change and Rights of

Evo Morales and the second coming of Túpaj Katari

There's a story Bolivians like to tell. It concerns an indigenous man called Julián Apaza, better known as Túpaj Katari.

One of three rebel leaders organizing resistance in different parts of the Spanish colony, in 1781 he gathered forces on the *altiplano* (high plain), on the rim of the deep bowl in which La Paz lies. From El Alto, where Túpaj Katari held court with his partner and comrade, Bartolina Sisa, the rebels laid siege to the city for 10 months.

Their aim was independence from Spain and social and racial equality; a cross-class, cross-race emancipation. This was an era of revolutionary ideas in France, North America and – though it rarely gets a mention in the history books – indigenous South America.

It almost worked. According to Spanish sources, the colonizers were within a hair's breadth of losing the Vice-Royalties of both Peru and Argentina during 1780 and 1781.

At first the rebels could count on the allegiance of creoles and mestizos who also wanted independence from Spain. But alliances broke down, support melted away. The rebellion was crushed and Túpaj Katari was executed most brutally. His arms and legs were attached to the tails of four horses which were made to pull in opposite directions. The quartered remains were displayed in different towns of the colony.

Who knows what might have happened had the indigenous-led rebellion been a success? Independence was to come 40 years later, led by creoles and mestizos, including Simón Bolívar. At first they too espoused ideals of equality. But within a short period the indigenous population were oppressed and exploited as before. Indian 'tribute' was restored and some two-thirds of the population denied citizenship.

Recently the indigenous-led bid for freedom and equality of the 1780s has had powerful resonances. Before he died, Túpaj Katari is reputed to have said: 'I will return, and I will be millions.' On assuming power as president of Bolivia in 2006, Evo Morales paid special tribute to the rebel Túpaj Katari, among others. To the millions of indigenous people watching and listening, it must have seemed that the moment of return had come. Not only had Evo Morales and the Movement Towards Socialism (MAS) party won the election – they had won by the largest majority in Bolivia's democratic history.

Vanessa Baird, *New Internationalist*, April 2008.

Reimagining the world

'The first step towards reimagining a world gone terribly wrong would be to stop the annihilation of those who have a different imagination – and imagination that is outside of capitalism as well as Communism. An imagination which has an altogether different understanding of what constitutes happiness and fulfillment. To gain this philosophical space, it is necessary to concede some physical space for the survival of those who may look like the keepers of our past but who may really be the guides to our future. To do this, we have to ask our rulers: Can you leave the water in the rivers, the trees in the forest? Can you leave the bauxite in the mountain?

Arundhati Roy, from *Broken Republic*, Hamish Hamilton 2011.

Mother Earth. Bolivia itself has approved what it calls the Law on Mother Earth, which, among other things, accords the status of 'personhood' to nature.

The picture has not been entirely rosy, even from an indigenous point of view. There has been much focus on the Framework Law on Autonomies, which it was thought would enable self-determination and territorial self-government by indigenous peoples in line with the new constitution. However, indigenous organizations felt they were being disregarded as the legislation was framed and this led to the first real indigenous protest against the Morales government, in the shape of the Sevenths Indigenous March on 21 June 2010.

Nevertheless, the importance of the Morales government for the indigenous movement within the Latin American region – and even in the world – remains. At least in part, the transformational impact of Morales has lain in his symbolic value rather than his achievements. According to Silvia Rivera, an Aymara professor of sociology at the University of San Andrés and co-founder of the Andean Oral History Workship: 'The main effect of having an indigenous president has been psychological. Evo's presence has altered the self-perception of being Indian. To be Indian is not to be miserable, poor, a beggar, but to be "knowing", to have political significance. It's a form of liberation, a recuperation of self-image, self-esteem.'[11]

Collectively, indigenous peoples are now a force to be reckoned with. They have scored major victories in the last 25 years. They have become highly visible and vocal, especially in the global justice movement where they have raised key questions about the social and ecological crisis that threatens the world. It was they who first alerted us all to our unsustainable relationship with 'Mother Earth' – and they were right. The 21st century is a new age of discovery, as those who were first 'discovered' explore and exercise their many strengths, and attempt to redress past wrongs.

The mood is summed up by a group of anti-nuclear activists, at whose core are Western Shoshone people, who declared on the eve of a protest at the US government's Nevada test site in Native American territory: '*Together… we will wise up, rise up, honor and resist.*'[12]

1 From *Fourth World Eye*, the online newsletter for the Center for World Indigenous Studies, No 11, February 2001. **2** IWGIA, *The Indigenous World 2011*, Copenhagen 2011. **3** From Beauclerk and Narby with Townsend, *Indigenous Peoples: a field-guide*. Part of this chapter draws upon this manual. **4** Written for this book by Victoria Geingos and Tommy A Busakhwe, members of the Hai || om and Khomani San groups respectively. **5** The workshop drew on a booklet that Anti-Slavery and the Minority Rights Group produced for the ILO, see Chandra Roy and Mike Kaye, 'The International Labour Organization: A Handbook for Minorities and Indigenous Peoples' (2002). This explains the workings of the ILO, how it can help defend and promote people's rights, and how indigenous and minority groups can work with it. **6** See *Indigenous Knowledge and Development Monitor* Vol 3, Issue 3 (December 1995), p 27. **7** Accessible at Forest Peoples Programme, nin.tl/n4VcZQ **8** From a talk given in Oxford, UK, Oct 2002. For more information, visit gcc.ca **9** Studies by H Gros Espiel and A Critescu, in Karen Parker, 'Understanding Self-Determination: The Basics', a presentation to the First International Conference on the Right to Self-Determination, UN, Geneva, August 2000, viewable at webcom.com/hrin/parker/selfdet.html **10** From 'Who are indigenous Africans?' at firstpeoples.org **11** Cited in *New Internationalist* 410, April 2008. **12** The Action for Nuclear Abolition and the Shundahai Network, protest at Nevada test site 5-12 October 2002, cited on firstpeoples.org

Contacts

INTERNATIONAL
Amnesty International amnesty.org
Anti-Slavery International antislavery.org
Center for World Indigenous Studies cwis.org
Cultural Survival culturalsurvival.org
Dana Declaration on Mobile Peoples and Conservation
    danadeclaration.org
First Peoples Worldwide firstpeoplesworldwide.org
Forest Peoples Programme forestpeoples.org
Indigenous Environmental Network ien.org
International Indian Treaty Council (IITC) treatycouncil.org
International Labour Organization (ILO) ilo.org
International Work Group for Indigenous Affairs (IWGIA) iwgia.org
Minority Rights Group International (MRG) minorityrights.org
Native Web nativeweb.org
Resource Centre for the Rights of Indigenous Peoples (GALDU)
    galdu.org
Survival International survivalinternational.org

AFRICA
First People of the Kalahari (Kgeikani Kweni) iwant2gohome.org
Indigenous Peoples of Africa Co-ordinating Committee (IPACC)
    ipacc.org.za
South African San Institute sasi.org.za
Working Group of Indigenous Minorities in Southern Africa (WIMSA)
    wimsanet.org

AUSTRALIA
Australian Institute of Aboriginal and Torres Strait Islander Studies
    (AIATSIS) aiatsis.gov.au
The Koori History Website kooriweb.org
Reconciliation Australia reconciliation.org.au

BRITAIN
African Initiatives african-initiatives.org.uk
Rainforest Foundation rainforestfoundationuk.org
Tourism Concern tourismconcern.org.uk

CANADA
Assembly of First Nations afn.ca
Defenders of the Land defendersoftheland.org
Indigenous Environmental Network ienearth.org
Inuit Tapiriit Kanatami itk.ca
Metis Cultural & Heritage Resource Centre metisresourcecentre.mb.ca

Indigenous media in Canada
Aboriginal Peoples Television Network (APTN) aptn.ca
Turtle Island News theturtleislandnews.com

EUROPE
European Network for Indigenous Australian Rights (ENIAR) eniar.org

NEW ZEALAND/AOTEAROA
Maori.org maori.org.nz
Peace Movement Aotearoa converge.org.nz/pma

UNITED STATES
American Indian Movement (AIM) aimovement.org
Honor the Earth honorearth.org
Kalahari Peoples Fund kalaharipeoples.org
National Congress of American Indians (NCAI) ncai.org
Native American Times nativetimes.com

Index

Index

Index